THE
ECONOMICS
OF THE
TOBACCO
INDUSTRY

THE
ECONOMICS
OF THE
TOBACCO
INDUSTRY

Paul R. Johnson

PRAEGER STUDIES IN
SELECT BASIC INDUSTRIES

PRAEGER SPECIAL STUDIES • PRAEGER SCIENTIFIC

New York • Philadelphia • Eastbourne, UK
Toronto • Hong Kong • Tokyo • Sydney

Library of Congress Cataloging in Publication Data

Johnson, Paul R. (Paul Reynold), 1929–
    The economics of the tobacco industry.

    Bibliography: p.
    Includes index.
    1. Tobacco industry—United States. I. Title.
HD9135.J63   1984   338.1'7371'0973   83-24503
ISBN 0-03-062562-9 (alk. paper)

Published in 1984 by Praeger Publishers
CBS Educational and Professional Publishing,
a Division of CBS Inc.
521 Fifth Avenue, New York, NY 10175 USA

Printed in the United States of America
on acid-free paper

PREFACE

Several of my colleagues have been asking me for some time to write a book about tobacco. A great deal of work on the economics of tobacco has been done in the Department of Economics and Business here at North Carolina State University. Much of the material is unpublished in masters theses and Ph.D. dissertations. Even the published material over the last 30 years is scattered, and it made sense to try to tie some of this material together.

I have been privileged to work for the Agricultural Experiment Stations in the two states that are the leading producers of the two major types of tobacco; flue-cured in North Carolina, and burley in Kentucky. I am sure my friends studying burley will feel that their product is slighted in this book. For many purposes the two products are identical. With minor exceptions, the support price programs are the same, and that subject is one of the major themes of the study. Where there are differences between the two tobaccos I have tried to point them out. The lack of more references to the excellent work on burley at the Universities of Kentucky and Tennessee is not intended to slight that work, the bibliography is extensive as it is, and some of the more general works cited contain references to those studies. The same comments apply to my colleagues' work on flue-cured at Clemson University, the University of Georgia, and Virginia Polytechnic Institute (VPI) and State University in Virginia. All of these institutions have ongoing research and extension programs concerning economic issues of tobacco.

Most of my research in recent years has been in international trade, with tobacco being only one of the products studied. This work, then, represents a substantial undertaking in certain of the areas covered. Certain colleagues here at N.C. State, and their counterparts at the other campuses mentioned, are walking encyclopedias of tobacco issues, policy, culture, and so on. I have relied heavily on two N.C. State colleagues over the years, as well as for the current work: Joe Chappell and Charles Pugh. Others who have been helpful in my education about tobacco are Robert Rudd, Milton Shuffet, W. D. Toussaint, Dale Hoover, and James Seagraves. I have received helpful comments on an earlier draft of the present work from T. J. Grennes, R. K. Perrin, and D. A. Sumner, as well as Chappell and Pugh.

The intended readership of this book falls into two groups. For the most part readers will no doubt be economists, however, much of the book is accessible to a more general reader. The most technical material is in Chapter 3 on supply control and Chapter 6 on international trade. The results of those analyses are summarized, and the general reader can omit the details. Other results are similarly described in a general fashion with the technical details omitted. The intent of the book is not to present any analytical breakthroughs; rather, it is to bring together some material on a commodity that is controversial in many ways, and has had some interesting economic problems associated with its production, manufacture, and consumption.

Since most economists believe that all markets are amenable to economic analysis, no matter how convoluted by government policy, I do not assert that the economics of tobacco is unique unto itself. Tobacco is an interesting commodity, however, with many features that distinguish it from other agricultural commodities. Those features are what motivated the writing of the book.

When I first started talking about this project, about four years ago, things were fairly tranquil in tobacco circles. The current (1983) problems were, perhaps, predictable, but had not really materialized. Tobacco had its foes, but they were less vocal it seemed; export markets, while not increasing, were not decreasing; imports were increasing, but the impact had not yet been felt; most important, the pressure on the supply control program had not intensified to its current level. So, while the intent all along was to discuss these issues and how they arose, they are now subjects of almost daily discussion in tobacco areas. Even so, no positions are taken on controversial matters like smoking and health. The author, for the nonce, smokes cigarettes.

CONTENTS

LIST OF TABLES

THE
ECONOMICS
OF THE
TOBACCO
INDUSTRY

1

INTRODUCTION

This book is concerned mainly with government policy and its effect on the production and marketing of tobacco. It is not intended to be a treatise on tobacco; it is, rather, a book concerned with analyzing certain economic phenomena. Tobacco is ideally suited to this kind of analysis, because it has few substitutes in production. With those characteristics, tobacco is easily isolated from other commodities, and the impact on quantities and prices from exogenous forces is more readily identifiable than it might be for other commodities.

While lengthy descriptions of various aspects of the tobacco industry are not necessary for the analysis that follows, certain background information will be useful. There are a number of extensive works that describe the nature of tobacco and delve into the history of the industry. These works are listed in the bibliography.

Types of Tobacco

There are three main types of tobacco produced in the United States—flue-cured, air-cured, and fire-cured. In addition, certain types of cigar leaf are also produced here. The types of tobacco and their use and relative importance are set out in Table 1.1. These types and numbers (Burley type 31, for example) are official designations of the U.S. Department of Agriculture. The first number essentially designates the curing method, 1 for flue-cured, 3 for air-cured, and so on. By far the most important tobaccos are flue-cured and

TABLE 1.1
Types of Tobacco and Production in 1978

Type	Production 1978 (million pounds)	Percentage of All Domestic Production
Flue-cured types 11–14	1,231	60.7
Burley type 31	626	30.9
Maryland type 32	31	1.5
Kentucky-Tennessee fire-cured type 22–23	51	2.5
Virginia fire-cured type 21	7	.3
Dark air-cured types 35–36	22	1.1
Sun-cured type 37	1	—
Pennsylvania Seedleaf filler	25	1.2
Ohio, Miami Valley filler types 42–44	3	.1
Puerto Rico filler type 46	3	.1
Connecticut Valley binder types 51–52	3	.1
Southern Wisconsin binder type 54	11	.5
Northern Wisconsin binder type 55	9	.4
Connecticut Valley Shade Grown type 61	4	.2

Source: U.S. Department of Agriculture. 1979. *Annual Report of Tobacco Statistics.*

burley. These tobaccos are the principal ingredients of cigarettes, which utilize over 90 percent of domestic manufacturing leaf.

Flue-cured tobacco is further broken down into four types, depending on where it is grown. The regions of production are known as belts. Type 11 is grown in the old and middle belts of Virginia and North Carolina; type 12 is grown in the new belt of eastern North Carolina; type 13 is grown in the border belt of North Carolina and South Carolina; type 14 is grown in the Georgia-Florida belt. The history of these belts will be traced briefly later.

Burley tobacco, an air dried type, has only one type—31. The bulk of the burley production is located in Kentucky and Tennessee, with approximately two-thirds of it grown in Kentucky. Smaller amounts are grown in West Virginia, Virginia, North Carolina, Ohio, and Indiana.

The third tobacco type used in domestic cigarette production is Maryland type 32. This tobacco is grown in Southern Maryland, and as we shall see, is unique in not having a price support program. This tobacco, like Burley, is an air-cured tobacco. While of relatively minor importance in terms of quantity, it is an important component of cigarette blends because of its slow burning.

There are three varieties of fire-cured tobaccos, Virginia type 21, and Kentucky-Tennessee types 22 and 23. These tobaccos are a principal ingredient of snuff, which, of course, has declined in consumption historically.

Two other tobaccos that have declined in importance since World War I are Dark air-cured types 35–36, and Virginia Sun-cured type 37. The former types are grown in Kentucky and Tennessee, while the latter is grown in Virginia. The main uses of these types have been in chewing tobacco, and small dark cigars; consumption of both of these has declined substantially.

Cigar leaf will play almost no role in the current study, but for completeness they will be listed here. There are three main types of cigar leaf—wrapper, filler, and binder. These are variously classed as types 41–62 for domestic U.S. tobacco. These tobaccos differ sharply from other tobaccos in their lack of government programs, methods of marketing, and even cultural practices in production. One interesting practice is the growing of cigar wrappers under cheesecloth or other cover, hence the name Shade Grown. This practice yields the superior leaf that is necessary for the wrapper use.

A Brief History of Tobacco

Tobacco has been produced in the United States from the earliest colonial times. Virginia, the site of the first permanent settlement, engaged in tobacco production essentially from the beginning. The use of tobacco by Indians, both in the Caribbean and North America, had been noted much earlier by the early explorers, including Columbus. The plant itself is native to the Western Hemisphere, but probably not native to Virginia. It was introduced to Europe by the Spanish in the sixteenth century. Sir Walter Raleigh introduced it into England in 1585. The first official written account concerning commerce in tobacco was in 1621, in Virginia (Herndon 1969).

Reliable data on tobacco production and consumption are not available for the colonial period in U.S. history (U.S. Department of Commerce 1960), however, some data are available on British imports of tobacco from 1616 on. Some of these import figures are shown in Table 1.2. Under the law for most of that time, England was to be the sole importer of tobacco from the colonies, so these figures are incomplete with respect to any tobacco that was smuggled to other destinations. Domestic consumption is also not recorded, however, close scrutiny of the data shows the growth in tobacco production throughout the colonial period.

The table also shows the colonial system at work. England (and later Scotland) would import the tobacco from the colonies and then reexport the tobacco to other destinations. Colonial exports of tobacco grew from a hundred thousand pounds in 1620 to a hundred million pounds just prior to the Revolutionary War. Without question, tobacco was the most important product exported from the colonies to England during this period. It was no accident, then, that Southern tobacco growers were sympathetic to the Revolution. They, like the tea importers, were subject to British taxes and what they perceived as capricious changes in those taxes. In addition, many tobacco growers financed their operations through loans from British merchants. Like all debtors, they felt that they were at the mercy of their creditors, and mistreated by them. Whether correct or not, this feeling led most of them to support the war. Following the war, they tried to have their debts repudiated, but were unsuccessful (see Robert 1967).

TABLE 1.2
Tobacco Imported by England and Reexports, Selected Colonial Years

Year	Imports (1,000 pounds)	Reexports (1,000 pounds)	Reexports as percentage of total
1620	119	NA	—
1630	458	NA	—
1672	17,559	NA	—
1686	23,036	NA	—
1697	36,000	18,000	50
1704	25,000	20,000	80
1710	23,000	15,000	65
1720	35,000	23,000	66
1730	41,000	27,000	66
1741	68,000	54,000	79
1752	78,000	69,000	88
1760	85,000	64,000	75
1771	105,000	87,000	83
1775	102,000	74,000	73

Source: U.S. Department of Commerce, Bureau of the Census. 1960.

Tobacco cultivation was the most important activity in the Virginia and Maryland colonies. So important was tobacco that it was used as a store of value, and at times as the unit of account. In the earliest colonial periods the landowners were English gentlemen who had received land grants from the British crown. The labor, other than the landowner, was by settlers, who often were indentured servants. The typical pattern for the indentured servants was to work out the indenture, and then move on to land of their own. Thus when slavery was introduced, the planters saw it as a more stable situation.

Slavery had been introduced into the British colonies for the production of sugar cane in the West Indies. The system moved to the North American colonies, where it was easily adapted to tobacco culture. Tobacco, then, was responsible for the establishment of the plantation system. A plantation was a more or less self contained unit. The major focus was on tobacco, which was the cash crop, mainly for export to England. Other crops were raised for food for the owners, overseers, and slaves, and for feed for animals.

At the same time that the plantation system was functioning, smaller operations by settlers were also viable. When tobacco production moved from the tidewater areas of Maryland and Virginia to piedmont Virginia and what was to become North Carolina, the plantation system was much less in evidence. Later, when tobacco culture moved across the mountains to Kentucky and Tennessee, it was even less dependent on slavery.

The Revolutionary War disrupted the colonial trade. Some tobacco got through the British blockade to other European countries, but trade was much disrupted. In fact, not only the Revolutionary War, but the Napoleonic Wars and the War of 1812 all disrupted the tobacco trade between the United States and Europe. It was not until after 1816 that trade in tobacco achieved the same level as before the Revolution.

Following the Revolution, tobacco culture crossed the Appalachian Mountains into Kentucky and Tennessee. Settlers in this area faced a new problem—how to get the tobacco marketed. At the time, Spain controlled the port of New Orleans and charged duty to load Kentucky and Tennessee tobacco on ocean-going vessels. What should have been a relatively easy route down the Ohio and Mississippi rivers was quite expensive. Contentious conditions among the settlers, Spain, and the U.S. government continued until 1795, when Spain granted free use of the Mississippi and the port of New Orleans. Of course, when Jefferson made the Lousiana Purchase in 1803, all of the territory now belonged to the United States and transportation was no longer an issue.

The early (colonial period) Virginia tobacco was a dark air-cured product. The major uses of tobacco at that time were snuff and smoking tobacco for pipes. As would be expected, Great Britain was the importer of almost all the Virginia Leaf. This import situation remained much the same in Virginia and Maryland for the 150 years before the Revolutionary War. As is normal for a colonial regime, some of the raw product came back as a manufactured product. In this case, snuff was reexported to the Eastern seaboard cities of what was to become the United States.

Meanwhile, the domestic market was to undergo a change and expansion. The principal use of tobacco in early colonial times had been pipe smoking, replaced in urban areas by snuffing. Chewing tobacco was thought fit only for sailors and certain physical laborers. After about 1820, chewing tobacco became much more prominent in all walks of life in the United States. This increase enlarged the production of tobacco and its domestic manufacture. With the exception of cigar leaf, production of tobacco now became concentrated in those areas where it is grown today. These areas were southern Maryland, Virginia, and North Carolina, and Kentucky and Tennessee. The product in all these areas, however, was different from the products of today. Whether air-cured, as in Maryland and Kentucky-Tennessee, or fire-cured, as was some of the Virginia crop, the tobacco was darker, rawer, and stronger than modern tobacco, especially modern blended cigarette tobacco.

The two major ingredients of the modern blended cigarette are flue-cured and burley tobacco. The other tobacco ingredients of lesser importance are Maryland, which improves the burning quality, and turkish, which is used as a flavor enhancer. Both flue-cured and burley tobaccos have interesting histories. Sometime around 1840 producers in the fire-cured areas of Virginia and North Carolina discovered that if the fire was outside the barn, and the heat conducted by a flue to the inside of the barn, a superior product emerged. The process was better controlled, and the operation itself was safer. The second feature that would make flue-cured tobacco a distinctive product was the color. As tobacco production moved to thinner and less fertile soils of the piedmont the cured leaf took on a lighter, yellowish color. When production moved to the even thinner soils of the coastal plain of North Carolina, this color change was even more pronounced. The tobacco thus came to be known as "bright leaf" tobacco. In addition to this color change, it was a milder tobacco when smoked.

Burley tobacco was a mutation, found in the 1860s, of the dark tobacco then being grown in Kentucky and Tennessee. It had a thinner leaf with great absorptive capacity. This feature made burley superior in its ability to hold flavorings, an especially desirable feature for chewing tobacco and later for blended cigarettes.

The Civil War split the tobacco growing region in half. Virginia, North Carolina, and Tennessee seceded while Maryland and Kentucky did not. Both sides thus had access to tobacco. The export trade of Virginia and North Carolina fell, while that of Kentucky increased.

Even though the plantation system of the southern United States originated in the growing of tobacco, by the time of the Civil War the plantation system was more closely associated with cotton culture. Tobacco culture was and is more labor intensive than cotton culture, but the fragility of the crop and the intricacies of the curing process limited the size of a manageable unit. Therefore, tobacco plantations were smaller than cotton plantations. Also, in Kentucky and Tennessee tobacco was largely grown on smaller farms operated by white freeholders.

While cotton was grown in North Carolina and even Virginia, it was not "King" as it was further south in Georgia, Alabama, Mississippi, and Louisiana. The invention of the cotton gin in 1793 had given the southern United States a comparative advantage in the production of cotton. Cotton production then developed on a grand scale. Plantations could be really quite large. Production on these units required many more slaves than a normal tobacco plantation. That part of the secessionist movement related to the slavery issue was much more important in the lower south than the upper south. Neither Virginia nor North Carolina were hotbeds of secessionists.

One sidelight of the war was the discovery by Northern troops of bright leaf tobacco. The last surrender of Southern troops took place at Durham Station, North Carolina, where the Northerners discovered a local smoking tobacco, Bull Durham, which then went on to national distribution and renown.

In the 1880s a cigarette making machine was perfected. Prior to that time cigarettes had been rolled by hand, as were cigars. Following the turn of the century cigarette consumption boomed. Cigarettes replaced chewing as the most popular form of tobacco consumption. Cigarette manufacturing was successfully monopolized; the monopoly was then broken up by the Supreme Court in 1911. This episode is described later.

During the first third of the twentieth century the production areas still present today were formed. Times were not always tranquil for tobacco farmers, however. Like farmers in general they went through cyclical price swings. Years or periods of low prices caused great anguish and much agitation. In 1907 and 1908, one particular episode in the dark tobacco and burley regions in Kentucky and Tennessee was associated with considerable violence and physical destruction. An attempt was made to restrict output in order to increase prices. Farmers who refused to join the association formed for this purpose were subject to raids by the "night riders." Whippings were administered and plant beds destroyed. The violence ultimately lessened, but the price fluctuations did not.

A sharp recession in 1921 affected all agricultural prices, including tobacco. The cooperative movement was quite popular at this time. Producers cooperatives had been formed in other areas. Such organizations would allocate production and marketing quotas for producers. Cooperatives were formed in the major tobacco areas. Their success was minimal at best, and they died out. Without any mechanism to ensure participation they had difficulty in controlling the marketing of tobacco. It was not until 1933, when the government control program came into being, that tobacco supply was controlled.

The more recent history of tobacco is taken up in detail later. The supply control program, the smoking and health issue, and international trade in tobacco are each dealt with as separate issues.

2

TOBACCO
MANUFACTURING

Introduction

Tobacco is chewed, sniffed, and smoked in various forms. Any of these forms requires processing of the tobacco from its state at harvest and first sale. Like the leaf itself, the manufacturing of tobacco products has changed through the years.

Tobacco is a storable product, in fact storage is necessary to age the product for cigarette manufacturing. Tobacco is not stable in its initial cured form, however. It is vulnerable to moisture fluctuations; if too dry it is brittle and shatters, if too wet it molds. In colonial times the tobacco was brought to a certain moisture level on the farm, then tightly packed in hogsheads for transport to market. At the central market the hogshead was opened, and the tobacco inside was inspected and sold. After sale the hogshead was re-sealed and the tobacco shipped to Great Britain or U.S. cities in a state that maintained the original moisture level.

In the current marketing system for flue-cured and burley tobaccos the method of sale is an auction. Farmers bring the cured leaf to a large warehouse. There the tobacco is graded and placed in individual piles in long rows. (This process is described later.) Each pile is sold separately, with the auctioneer and the buyers walking along the row, halting briefly at each pile. The auctioneer starts the bidding and then the price is bid up until the pile is sold.* These buyers represent cigarette manufactures, exporters, and consignment buyers. The selling of cigarette leaf occurs over a period of about nine months. Flue-cured markets open in late July and close in November; burley markets open in December and close in February. Maryland tobacco is sold in the spring after the burley markets are closed. In general, the same buyers purchase all three types of tobacco, and the same auctioneers sell the three types. The buyers of the tobacco move the tobacco to a nearby assembly point where it is packed into hogsheads. These hogsheads are then moved to an elaborate redrying facility. There the tobacco can be sorted, cleaned, and brought to the proper moisture level. It is then repacked by grade into hogsheads and stored for the aging process. Thus, there is a continuous inventory of various grades and varieties of tobacco on hand in company warehouses. This tobacco is available for whatever end use desired.

Currently, cigarette manufacture uses the greatest amount of tobacco. Since it has not always been so, some description of other uses will be made. The cigarette industry will then be examined in a little more detail.

---

*In Canada, tobacco is sold in a Dutch auction. This type of auction is started at a price above that expected to prevail. The price is then allowed to fall until someone stops the auction with a bid. In a regular auction, the successful buyer knows his competitors' stopping prices, while in a Dutch auction he can only anticipate them. This latter auction presumably favors the seller.

Smoking, Chewing, and Snuffing

In addition to cigarettes, tobacco is smoked in pipes and as cigars. These were the traditional ways of smoking until the late nineteenth century. Cigarette manufacture was a hand operation until a workable machine was developed in the early 1880s. Before the turn of the century tobacco production was a small-scale manufacturing process.

Smoking and chewing tobacco were made from tobacco that had been cured, redried and destemmed, and then aged. Chewing tobacco can take several forms: Plug tobacco is a dense, tightly wrapped, small-sized unit of tobacco from which a quantity can be cut for chewing. So-called scrap chewing tobacco is made of loose pieces of tobacco, which can be taken directly from a package for chewing purposes. Smoking tobacco was historically roughly the same product as chewing tobacco, except that the product was shredded and crimped for smoking. Snuff, on the other hand, had to be ground into a very fine powdery form for use. Historically, snuff was consumed by inhaling it through the nostrils. Current U.S. usage is to place the material against the gum in the mouth. One tobacco product, twist, was used either for smoking or chewing, and was a common form of home consumption of tobacco.

Two interesting events in the history of U.S. tobacco consumption occurred in the 1940s. It was only after World War II that cuspidors disappeared from U.S. Post Offices and other public buildings. Their presence attested to the widespread use of chewing tobacco in urban, as well as rural areas. Their disappearance confirmed the long downward trend in chewing. The second event was that snuff consumption increased during the war, reversing another downward trend. Consumption returned to its normal level after the war. This reversal is attributed to the prohibition of smoking in munitions and other defense facilities, causing a substitution away from cigarettes to other forms of tobacco consumption.

Until the advent of the cigarette, cigar manufacturing was the only process where a particular hand-product was produced. Not only was cigar tobacco production more widely dispersed than the other smoking and chewing tobaccos, but so was the manufacturing process. Historically, this was a small-scale, hand-product process. Currently, like cigarettes, cigars are machine made and the scale of a plant is much larger. Tobacco consumption in cigars, however, is only a small fraction of that in cigarettes. As noted earlier, the production of cigar leaf is not subject to the same supply controls as cigarette leaf production, and the whole industry is less interesting as an economic problem than cigarettes.

The Modern Cigarette Industry

Cigarette manufacturing in the United States has a colorful history with many interesting personalities. There have been many studies of tobacco, cigarettes, and the people involved. The material here is essentially a synopsis of these other published works, and an updating of some of the data concerning cigarette manufacturing.

Two incidents in the history of cigarette manufacturing play a significant role in interest in and information about the industry. There were two anti-trust cases brought under the Sherman Anti-Trust Act. The first case involved a settlement breaking up the tobacco trust in 1911. The second was a criminal trial in 1941, which resulted in a guilty verdict. The Supreme Court upheld this verdict in 1946. This second trial produced a voluminous record and provided data and information on the industry that had not been available previously. Three book-length studies of tobacco and cigarette pricing were produced by economists from this information (Jackson 1955, Nicholls 1951, Tennant 1950).

The Supreme Court verdict in 1946 involved new precedent in anti-trust law, and the economics studies were attempts to sort out the economic facts of the case. Since these studies are available, there is no need to redo their work. Thirty years have passed since those studies were made, however, and what were current data are no longer so. More interesting, the anti-trust issue no longer appears so intriguing, and is not an issue of importance at the moment.

Washington Duke and Sons, a Durham, North Carolina firm, was one of the first to install the new cigarette-making machinery. Through aggressive selling and pricing policies, especially by James B. Duke, the Duke firm became the American Tobacco Company through acquisition of its largest competitors, and by 1889 had over 90 percent of cigarette sales. The Dukes then consolidated their tobacco holdings by merging some of the larger smoking and chewing tobacco firms into the trust.

The original form of the tobacco trust was a holding company of interlocking directorates, the classic combination at which the Sherman Anti-Trust Act was targeted. To avoid the antitrust problems the holding company was converted to a single entity, the American Tobacco Company. That move was not successful, and the company was prosecuted under the Sherman Act. The case ended up in the Supreme Court, where the decision was that the trust be broken up or barred from interstate commerce. Under the decree, the American Tobacco Company and its affiliates were broken up into four major domestic companies: a new American Tobacco Company, Liggett and Meyers, R. J. Reynolds, and Lorillard. Reynolds, which later was to be a leader in cigarette manufacture, received no cigarette business in the split. In addition, the two foreign parts of the tobacco trust, Imperial and British American, were split off and came under British and not U.S. control. Subsequently, Imperial gained monopoly power for cigarette manufacturing in Great Britain, while British American took over overseas operations in British colonies and elsewhere. Interestingly, both companies resumed some operations in the United States. Imperial established processing plants to perform the first stages of their cigarette manufacturing process closer to the source of the U.S. tobacco they were buying. They shut down the last of their plants in the late 1970s. British American, now BAT Industries, owns Brown and Williamson, a major U.S. manufacturer of cigarettes.

As can be seen from Tables 2.1 and 2.2 the years following the 1911 decree saw an enormous growth in the output of cigarettes. American, Liggett and Meyers, and Reynolds had the largest shares of this market. By the twenties the companies were concentrating their large advertising budgets on single brands: Lucky Strike (American), Camel (Reynolds), and Chesterfield (Liggett and Meyers). The companies were engaged in a fierce competitive battle, based on advertising rather than prices. The size of the corporations, their continued profitability during the depression, their small number, and the identical prices all contributed to renewed suspicion of conspir-

TABLE 2.1
Manufactured Tobacco Products, Selected Years 1870–1930

Year	Manufactured Tobacco and Snuff (million pounds)	Cigars (millions)	Cigarettes (millions)
1870	102	1,183	16
1875	124	1,828	56
1880	146	2,510	533
1885	207	3,294	1,080
1890	253	4,229	2,505
1895	274	4,099	4,238
1900	301	5,566	3,870
1905	368	6,748	4,477
1910	447	6,810	9,782
1915	442	6,599	18,945
1920	413	8,097	48,091
1925	414	6,463	82,712
1930	372	5,894	124,193

Source: U.S. Department of Commerce, Bureau of the Census. 1960.

acy among the companies. The 1930s saw a renewed interest in "trust busting" in general, and the cigarette companies were vulnerable to this effort.

The suspicions culminated in the bringing of a suit by the Justice Department against the major companies and their officers on criminal charges under the Sherman Act in 1941 (United States v. American Tobacco Co. U.S. District Court for the Eastern District of Kentucky). Technically, the charges were for the crime of conspiracy. A jury found the companies and their officers guilty after a trial that lasted almost five months. The verdict was appealed and a Supreme Court decision in 1946 upheld the conviction. The case was considered important by both lawyers and economists.

As noted earlier, the case provided information for economic analysis. An interesting feature of the case is that monopoly power in two markets was alleged. Tobacco companies were said to have conspired in the buying of tobacco at the warehouse—monopsonistic behavior. They were also accused of conspiring in the selling of cigarettes—monopolistic behavior. The three book-length studies mentioned failed to find evidence of this kind of behavior in an *economic* sense. That is, in the absence of formal collusion, which was not proven, there was no evidence that the companies were restricting output and raising prices for cigarettes. Neither is there evidence that the companies were restricting purchases and lowering prices for tobacco on a sustained basis.

The case is also interesting, from a legal standpoint. The case was tried in Lexington, Kentucky, in the heart of the burley producing region. This made jury selection difficult, and is mentioned in a concurring opinion in the 1946 decision (Robert 1967). The Supreme Court decision broke new legal ground with the novel doctrine of "conscious parallelism." (This term was not used in the 1946 decision but in a later case.) The court judged the case on the narrow ground of whether actual exclusion of competitors is necessary for a violation of the Sherman Act, or if simply the power to do so is sufficient. The court held for the latter view and the lower court convictions were upheld.

Two observations on pricing were at the heart of the government case. In 1931 the major companies increased the price of cigarettes at the same time the price of the raw material, tobacco, was declining. Second, the pattern of wholesale cigarette prices was the same for all the companies. The 1931 observation is not sufficient in itself to prove collusion on either side of the market. On the observed pricing pattern, one need only note that the same price for the same product is as true of competitive markets as it is of cartel markets. Therefore, it can fairly be said that the court's case is not supported by purely economic reasoning.

In any event, there was little change in the production or distribution of cigarettes as a result of the decision. That is, if there was cartel behavior in 1941, there were no more firms engaged in cigarette production 35 years later. The market share of the various companies has changed markedly, however (see Table 2.3). In 1949, the three major cigarette makers were American, with 31 percent of the domestic market, Reynolds, with 26 percent, and Liggett and Meyers, with 20 percent (Tennant 1950). By 1979, Liggett and Meyer's share had fallen to about 2 percent. The leader in terms of sales was

TABLE 2.2
Cigars, Cigarettes, Chewing Tobacco, Smoking Tobacco, and Snuff Manufactured in the United States, averages 1919–53, annual 1956–81

Year	Cigars (million)	Cigarettes (million)	Chewing Tobacco (mil. lbs.)	Smoking Tobacco (mil. lbs.)	Snuff (mil. lbs.)
1919–23 Avg.	7,113.6	55,022.8	145.2	229.8	36.3
1924–28 Avg.	6,490.3	91,113.5	123.0	242.0	39.2
1929–33 Avg.	5,288.6	116,952.7	147.0	177.0	38.8
1934–38 Avg.	4,940.3	154,098.4	114.0	193.5	37.1
1939–43 Avg.	5,449.4	228,333.4	108.8	188.7	39.9
1944–48 Avg.	5,444.8	352,459.0	109.2	125.4	41.1
1949–53 Avg.	5,637.2	410,867.3	86.5	100.1	39.7
1956	5,766.6	424,246.2	75.7	71.5	37.7
1957	5,902.9	442,327.4	72.4	70.5	36.1
1958	6,225.4	470,067.5	69.3	76.0	34.8
1959	6,608.4	489,864.8	68.1	73.2	34.3
1960	6,768.1	506,944.2	64.9	73.8	34.6
1961	6,454.5	528,332.4	65.2	74.2	33.8
1962	6,597.7	535,495.7	64.7	70.9	33.2
1963	6,652.6	550,558.3	65.1	70.4	31.8
1964	8,727.9	539,907.8	66.2	82.4	31.4
1965	7,899.5	556,806.1	65.1	71.8	29.7
1966	7,165.3	567,264.5	65.2	67.3	29.5
1967	6,858.9	576,182.6	64.4	64.8	29.3

18

1968	7,184.2	597,492.9	65.4	66.3	27.1
1969	6,937.1	557,646.6	69.8	63.9	27.6
1970	7,094.7	583,250.2	68.8	69.4	26.5
1971	6,721.9	576,424.8	71.4	60.5	26.4
1972	6,024.8	599,069.6	72.6	55.8	25.5
1973	5,664.2	644,245.0	74.0	53.0	25.3
1974	5,293.6	635,016.8	79.2	49.0	25.0
1975	4,524.2	651,211.0	81.5	46.2	24.4
1976	4,236.1	693,389.4	83.6	44.6	24.8
1977	3,907.0	665,864.2	89.0	40.7	24.6
1978	3,795.5	695,990.9	94.6	36.4	25.1
1979	3,600.6	704,243.4	102.3	32.8	23.7
1980	3,454.4	714,307.1	106.0	32.2	24.3
1981	3,428.1	734,703.0	106.3	30.3	26.0

Source: U.S. Department of Agriculture. Various years. Annual Report of Tobacco Statistics.

19

Reynolds, with 33 percent, followed by Philip Morris, with 29 percent, and Brown and Williamson, with 14 percent, while American had fallen to 11 percent (Overton 1981).

The smoking and health issue, to be discussed in Chapter 4, had a lot to do with this shaking up of the cigarette industry. The old standard brands of unfiltered cigarettes were no longer the preferred smoke. In the 1950s, filtered cigarettes picked up rapidly; the Marlboro Man became a fixture on television. "Winston Tastes Good Like a Cigarette Should," not only put English teachers in a frenzy, it also sold lots of cigarettes. Philip Morris and Reynolds were aggressive marketers of their own brands. American and Liggett and Meyers were not as successful in attracting smokers to their competing brands, and their share of the market headed downward. After the Surgeon General's Report in 1964, tars in cigarette smoke became an issue. The response of the manufacturers was to advertise low tar content. Again, in the 1970s, Philip Morris and Reynolds were aggressive in these new markets, and by 1980 were the dominant firms sharing over 60 percent of the market between them.

Another interesting development was taking place in the 1960s among cigarette manufacturers. By 1972, no domestic cigarette company was entirely dependent on tobacco for revenue. Even the leaders, Reynolds and Philip Morris, were into such things as food, transportation, and beer. Actual consumption of cigarettes had not declined, and cigarette making was still profitable. The handwriting was on the wall, however, and the cigarette companies used their sizable cash flows to acquire and/or merge with nontobacco companies. By 1979, domestic tobacco accounted for 64 percent of Reynold's net earnings, down from 81 in 1972. Cigarettes accounted for 15 percent of Liggett and Meyers's net earnings, down from 42 percent in 1973. The other companies were somewhere between these two percentages (Overton 1981).

Is There Now or Was There Ever a Cartel?

Industrial organization specialists use a variety of measures to gauge market performance. One usually easily computed measure is the concentration ratio. This ratio is simply the percentage of sales (or some other output measure) that is controlled by the top four (or some other arbitrary number) firms. By this measure the domestic cigarette industry is highly concentrated now, and was in the 1940s. The four largest firms in 1940 controlled 81.4 percent of the domestic cigarette market; in 1979 the four largest firms controlled 87.7 percent of the market. As noted above, however, these four firms were not the same in the two years. Brown and Williamson had replaced Liggett and Meyers in the group, and Philip Morris had moved from fourth place to second. This information on structure does not really tell us much about behavior. What we need to know is whether there is anticompetitive behavior that is adversely affecting the economy. We need evidence that price is above marginal cost to the industry and its firms. Such evidence would be a necessary, but not sufficient, condition for anticompetitive behavior. The resulting cost to the economy, of course, would be an inefficient use of resources. Before turning to a recent, ingenious attempt to secure the evidence by Daniel Sumner, we need a little more descriptive data about the industry.

An anomalous fact is that despite being found guilty of a Sherman Act violation, nothing really changed in the behavior of the major cigarette manufacturers. This result is consistent with the failure of the three studies mentioned in the first part of this chapter to find economic evidence of collusive behavior. With the hindsight of 30 years, the studies make interesting reading. Each starts as if the author were saying, "Given the court decision, and given all these data, I will come up with the villains for you." Each ends with the author more or less saying; "I have pored over some interesting data and anecdotes from the trial, but I cannot put my finger on the villains." How do we explain this outcome?

The evidence is clear to the most casual observer that at the retail level for any given market (taxes vary by state) the price of cigarettes is the same across brands. But the retailing and wholesaling links in the chain of distribution can almost be taken as prima facie evidence of competition. There is an almost endless number of retail outlets. There is a large number of wholesalers in various markets and no apparent barriers to entry. The question, then, is whether the manufacturers can set prices so that despite competition at the distribution level the price is above marginal cost.

Some mention should be made of the changing market shares and changing brand loyalties. These changes through time were shown in Table 2.3. The cigarette manufacturers have been fierce competitors for market share. (The effect of advertising on the industry as a whole as opposed to individual brands is discussed in Chapter 4. Here, we are concerned with brand loyalties.) From the 1920s to 1950 each company was concentrating on one brand to promote, and large advertising expenditures were being made to convince smokers to switch. The new medium of radio was a perfect tool for this task. Enormous amounts of resources were spent and the share of the three largest selling cigarettes, Lucky Strike, Camel, and Chesterfield, did appear to be fairly stable from the late 1920s to World War II.

After 1950, as noted earlier, the cigarette market was turned upside down. Concern over the health issue resulted first in filter cigarettes, then low tar cigarettes. The technology of manufacturing cigarettes changed; less tobacco per cigarette was used, the mix of various tobaccos could be changed, and other developments took place. The change in the kind of cigarette produced new brand names, and brand loyalties changed. Since the loyalty was to a brand and not the company, the fortunes of the companies changed. Since market shares were being affected, quite drastically in some cases, the cartel case is much less compelling after 1950.

The advertising wars continued unabated, although a forced shift in media took place in 1971. This advertising activity was designed to retain and/or attract new market share for particular brands. One thing that economists have long agreed on is that for a cartel to continue successfully, an enforceable market-sharing agreement is necessary. Again, with hindsight, it is difficult to believe a price-fixing cartel was operating when the major participants were spending so much to change the market shares. It is doubtful that there will be much public concern about cartel activity among cigarette manufacturers in the future. This prediction is supported by the fact that the companies are now all conglomerates and less dependent on cigarettes for revenue. It is also buttressed by a recent empirical study.

Sumner (1981) developed an innovative way to examine the price versus marginal cost question. Since each state taxes cigarettes

TABLE 2.3
Market Share of U.S. Domestic Cigarette Sales (in percent)

Year	Reynolds	Philip Morris	Brown and Williamson	American Brands	Lorillard	Liggett and Meyers
1913	0.2	n/a	n/a	35.3	22.1	34.1
1925	41.6	0.5	n/a	21.2	1.9	26.6
1930	28.6	0.4	0.2	37.6	6.9	25.0
1939	23.7	7.1	10.6	23.5	5.8	21.6
1940	21.7	9.6	7.8	29.5	5.4	20.6
1949	26.3	9.2	5.9	31.3	5.0	20.2
1955	25.8	8.5	10.5	32.9	6.1	15.6
1960	32.1	9.4	10.4	26.1	10.6	11.3
1965	32.6	10.5	13.3	25.7	9.2	8.7
1970	31.8	16.8	16.9	19.3	8.7	6.5
1975	32.5	23.8	17.0	14.2	7.9	4.4
1979	32.7	29.0	14.5	11.5	9.6	2.7

Source: Tennant 1950; Overton 1981.

at its own rate there is a distribution of prices that is both cross sectional and through time. Given the legal barriers and the physical distances involved, these tax differentials cannot be eliminated by arbitrage. Therefore, Sumner argues, if certain aggregation issues are met a firm level demand elasticity can be estimated. His reasoning makes the aggregation argument highly plausible so that one can place quite a bit of confidence in his numbers.

Actually, Sumner rejects both the hypothesis of atomistic competition in cigarette manufacturing and the hypothesis of monopoly power. This second rejection is based on his estimates of firm-level demand elasticities that range downward from about -13.5. This means that the demand curves that firms face are quite flat, negating firm-level market power. These elasticities compare to an industry-level elasticity of about -0.4. Any effect on cigarette prices is probably less than 5 percent.

Given this empirical evidence in conjunction with the structural change in the industry, it seems safe to say that the cigarette cartel problem is behind us. Some firm or group of firms currently making cigarettes may be accused of anticompetitive behavior, but it will not be related to cigarettes.

3

WELFARE IMPLICATIONS OF SUPPLY CONTROL

Introduction

The supply control program for tobacco has been on the books since 1933. There have been many technical changes in the program's operation. These changes and their effects will be discussed later in the chapter. First, however, the general nature of supply control programs and the nature of gains and losses will be described.

The demand function for most agricultural products is inelastic, which, of course, means that an increase in price will increase total revenue to the industry. Each individual producer is a price taker, so unless his output is cut too sharply, he also gains from a price increase. Throughout the 1920s, agricultural prices in general were perceived to be depressed relative to other prices. There were several price raising schemes proposed during that decade; none of them was put into action. The groundwork had been laid, however, for output controls to be employed when the Great Depression arrived in the 1930s. The first such scheme to become law was the Agricultural Adjustment Act of 1933 (AAA), whose stated attempt was to achieve parity for agricultural producers. Parity was defined as a price sufficient to achieve the same ratio of prices received by farmers to prices paid by farmers that had existed in some earlier period. For nontobacco products controlled by the AAA this earlier period was 1910–14; for tobacco it was August 1919 to July 1929. The increased price was to be achieved by restricting output. Since all programs that followed that of 1933 are some variant of a basic supply control program, some general principles can be discussed before getting into specific programs.

Figure 3.1 can be used to analyze the social gains and losses from controlling output of tobacco. Looking first at panel (c) and considering first the lower supply schedule mi, we get the standard textbook welfare analysis. The demand curve in panel (c) is the total demand curve facing domestic producers of tobacco. If output is restricted from Q'' to Q' then the price will be raised from a free market equilibrium price of P'' to the price P'. Employing the concepts of consumer and producer surplus, the welfare calculations are straightforward, although not without controversy. A brief discussion and justification is contained in the appendix to this chapter.

The opportunity cost of resources used to produce tobacco is given by the supply curve. Resources valued at $Q'Q''$ji are released from tobacco production to go into another use. Consumers move up the demand curve from i to g. Consumers' surplus in the amount $gP'P''$h is transferred to producers of tobacco. That leaves a net social loss of gji, where ghi is lost consumer surplus and hij is lost producer surplus. That is not the end of the story for tobacco, however. Restricting attention now to flue-cured tobacco, the United States has substantial market power in export markets for flue-cured tobacco. This market power stems largely from a quality differential that is analyzed in Chapter 6. For current purposes assume this power exists and is stable.

By well known principles in international trade theory a nation (or industry) can actually improve national income at the expense of

FIGURE 3.1
Social welfare areas of flue-cured tobacco program

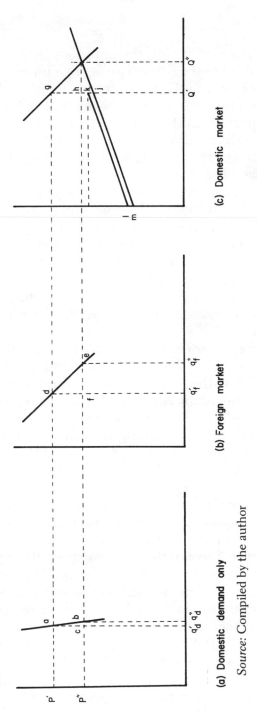

(a) Domestic demand only

(b) Foreign market

(c) Domestic market

Source: Compiled by the author

27

its trading partners. This is the optimum tariff argument. For U.S. flue-cured tobacco the support price program acts as an excise tax on the export of tobacco. This price wedge and a less than perfectly elastic demand curve for exports means that more revenue is being earned from the export of tobacco than would have to be spent on resources to acquire the domestic value of the equivalent imports. In other words, we are collecting rents from foreign buyers. Since social cost calculations are measures of what happens to national income we have to make two adjustments to the areas depicted in panel (c).

Part of the triangle ghi, lost consumer surplus, is taken from foreign consumers of flue-cured tobacco. This is not part of national income from the U.S. point of view. In adding up costs and returns from the program, then, the area labeled def in panel (b) can be ignored. From a global standpoint this area is lost from world income; the optimum tariff is always secured at someone's expense. Since we are only concerned with domestic income, we will omit def from the calculations.

The more important area is $dfP''P'$ in panel (b). This area is a transfer from foreign consumers to domestic producers of flue-cured tobacco. This is the revenue that constitutes a net rent collected from foreign buyers by virtue of the market (or monopoly) power on the part of the United States. This revenue is a positive gain in terms of national income accounting. As long as the U.S. price is held above the competitive price, export sales at that price will generate these rents. Two sidelights concerning these rents are worth mentioning. An excise tax on exports is unconstitutional in the United States. So even if the nation enjoys monopoly power in certain areas it cannot take advantage of that power directly. Therefore, while the tobacco program has exactly the same effect as an export tax, it is not an explicit tax. Second, the proceeds from the monopoly rents accrue directly to the producers of tobacco. The proceeds from a tariff or tax in general accrue to the U.S. Treasury, the subsequent transfers are a separate item. In the case of the program the transfers are direct and immediate.

The area $acP''P'$ in panel (a) is the domestic transfer to producers from consumers. Historically in this kind of welfare analysis, areas of this kind have been ignored. Distributional considerations are set aside as they require interpersonal utility considerations. In the present case transfers are being made from consumers to allotment holders, but economic analysis has nothing to say about this. In the last decade or so these transfers have gotten renewed attention, not for utility comparisons, but because they also represent potential social loss.

Three articles by Krueger (1974), Posner (1975), and Tullock (1967) called attention to the fact that these transfers are valuable assets and economic agents will spend resources to acquire or keep them. This activity has become known as "rent seeking." The general setting for the phenomenon is as follows: The Congress considers a new tariff, for example. This tariff will produce returns to domestic producers of the good. Once in place, those returns will be a valuable asset of the firms producing the product. These firms then have an incentive to spend resources to acquire this asset through lobbying and similar activities. Second, after the tariff is in place the firms have an incentive to keep spending resources to keep the asset. The logic here is certainly unexceptionable; even the most casual observer can see this rent-seeking activity taking place not only in the United States but around the world. The next step, however, stated most clearly by Posner and Tullock, raises some measurement problems.

These writers contend that the whole transfer rectangle acP^*P' is a social cost to be added to the usual welfare triangle. They argue that rent seeking is competitive, and that people engaged in that activity will spend resources to the point that the marginal cost of seeking rents equals the marginal revenue from that activity. This equilibrium condition would mean that the whole rectangle would be spent on rent seeking—a socially wasteful activity. Ultimately, of course, there is an empirical problem to be resolved as to the magnitude of rent seeking; there are also some theoretical issues concerning the basic concepts of measuring waste. Suffice it to say here that some analysts would add the rectangle as an additional loss of restricting output of flue-cured tobacco.

Table 3.1 contains some estimates of these social costs and gains in 1965 and in 1980. The 1965 calculations will be discussed at greater length in Chapter 6. These results were obtained from a 1965 study in which the possibility of monopoly gains accruing were first discussed (Johnson 1965). The 1980 calculations come from a 1981

TABLE 3.1
Social Costs of the Flue-Cured Tobacco Program
in Millions of Dollars, 1965 and 1980

	1965(I)	1965(II)	1980	1980[a] (1965 prices)
U.S. consumer surplus	– 4.1	– 4.1	– 1.8	– 0.7
Net producer surplus	– 12.0	– 12.0	– 24.3	– 9.3
Efficiency loss	– 25.0	– 79.9	– 48.0	– 18.4
Monopoly rent	48.0	48.0	113.9	43.7
U.S. social welfare	7.5	– 48.0	39.9	15.3
Rest of World (ROW)				
consumer surplus	– 5.2	– 5.2	– 18.8	– 7.2
World social welfare	– 46.3	– 101.2	– 92.9	– 35.5
Domestic transfer			128.5	49.2

[a]Adjusted by the Consumer Price Index.
Source: Compiled by the author

Ph.D. dissertation (Norton 1981). Calculating the areas in Figure 3.1 depends critically on the elasticities of demand and supply, and by how much the price is fixed above the competitive level (the issue of the demand elasticity estimate is discussed in Chapter 6). For 1980 the price is calculated to be 16.7 percent above the competitive level. The necessary demand elasticities have been estimated from a three equation, three stage least squares procedure. The domestic demand elasticity was estimated to be – .2, and the foreign demand elasticity to be – 2.3. The domestic supply elasticity is taken to be 1.0.

Two columns are shown for 1980; one is in current dollars, the other in 1965 dollars to make the two studies comparable. For current purposes it is only necessary to look at the 1980 prices. The area acb in Fig. 3.1, lost consumer surplus, is not very big—$1.8 million. There is some net producer surplus lost from restricting output, hij, that is estimated to be $24.3 million. The revenue transferred to producers from domestic activity, of course, is larger than this loss. The last item in the column shows this transfer to be five times the lost producer surplus. The efficiency loss, the area lhjm in panel (c), is $48 million. This loss is due to the program's restriction of the area in which tobacco can be grown. The great difference between 1965 and 1980 in the efficiency loss will be discussed later. The inefficiencies remaining in 1980 are due to the fact that tobacco allotments cannot be leased across county lines.

The next item listed is monopoly rent. This is the rectangle dfP*P' in panel (b). This revenue is that collected from foreign buyers above the opportunity cost of the resources used. Since it is counted as positive the national accounts and it exceeds the domestic resource and utility losses, the next item shows the program yielded on an annual basis in 1980 dollars a gain of approximately $40 million.

In recent years imports of flue-cured tobacco have increased fairly sharply. Public information is scant about the quality and other attributes of this tobacco. Therefore, little is known about whether U.S. importers are able to exercise market power on that side of the market. Also, much less Burley tobacco is exported; therefore, the domestic consumer and producer loss in that area is greater than any monopoly rents. The domestic transfer will also be larger. Taking rounded numbers for illustrative ease, if the price is 20 percent above the competitive level, and domestic marketings are 500 million pounds, then the transfer to domestic allotment holders is in the neighborhood of $175 million. The total domestic rents that the program is transferring is about $300 million. With these general notions of magnitude, and analysis of costs and returns, we can turn to a historical review of the program and its changes through time.

The Early Years of the Tobacco Program

As noted, tobacco was included in the original Agricultural Adjustment Act as a commodity whose price was to be supported. There are several useful works that treat in some detail not only the AAA but the role of tobacco in it. A recent and interesting treatment is a history of the period, *Prosperity Road, The New Deal, Tobacco and North Carolina* (Badger 1980). This study is a political history of the flue-cured tobacco program. An earlier treatment, closer to the scene, was one of the Brookings Institution monographs on the

AAA, *Tobacco Under the AAA* (Rowe 1935). A North Carolina State University study, *Flue Cured Tobacco Programs 1933-1958* (Brooks and Williamson 1958) treats the early years as well as some post war developments. The current treatment will be much condensed from these studies. The emphasis will be on the economic implications of the various changes in the program.

The Agricultural Adjustment Act was passed after the 1933 tobacco crop had been planted. There was thus no machinery in place to affect the price of the 1933 crop. The price remained depressed relative to the prices that prevailed before 1931. The governor of North Carolina ordered the tobacco markets closed until an agreement could be reached between growers and buyers. A campaign was started to get growers to agree to limit output the next year. In short order, 95 percent of the growers agreed to do so. With this agreement in hand, the secretary of agriculture met with the major tobacco manufacturers. These manufacturers in turn agreed to take the same amount of the 1933 crop that they had taken of the 1932 crop at an average price of 17 cents per pound. When buying resumed, the price achieved this level. It had been 10 cents per pound before trading had been suspended. The season average price finished at 15.3 cents up from 11.6 in 1932. Growers who had sold before the agreement were compensated for the price difference by the Agricultural Adjustment Administration. The funds were collected by taxes levied on processors, holders of inventory, and imports.

The program was in operation for the 1934 crop. Each tobacco farm was given a base acreage that was determined by one of several alternative measures of the recent production for that farm. The secretary of agriculture determined that 70 percent of the total base acreage would yield the desired supply to maintain the price of tobacco. Each farm then was given an acreage allotment and a production allotment of 70 percent of its base. The remaining 30 percent of the base was rented to the secretary at the rate of $17.50 per acre. The growers also received an adjustment payment based on production. Growers with four acres or more received 12.5 percent of the value of the production allotment; growers with less than four acres received a slightly higher payment. The grower was also eligible for a deficiency payment if actual production fell below the allotment production.

A potential loophole existed in the 1934 program. A non-cooperator could produce as much tobacco as he chose and take advantage of the higher price that would result from the program. To forestall this possibility Congress passed the Kerr Tobacco Act in June 1934. This act placed a tax of up to 33.3 percent of the sales price, at time of sale, for noncooperators. As a result of the program, production was down sharply and the price increased to 27.3 cents per pound.

In January 1936, the Supreme Court invalidated sections of the Agricultural Adjustment Act of 1933 in the Hoosac Mills case. The Congress promptly repealed the Kerr Tobacco Act. Thus, the original AAA program was really in effect only for the 1934 and 1935 crop years.

Congress passed the Soil Conservation and Domestic Allotment Act of 1936, essentially as an emergency action. The act called for payment to farmers for diverting acreage from soil depleting crops to soil conserving ones. Since most of the crops, including tobacco, that were included in the 1933 legislation were classed as soil depleting they were eligible for payment under the new legislation.

The soil conservation program was quite simple. Farmers were to be paid 5 cents a pound for production diverted from tobacco. The expectation, of course, was that enough production would be diverted that the market price would increase from where it would otherwise have been. There was no penalty for not participating in the program. If a farmer was participating in the program for other crops he could be penalized 5 cents a pound for pounds of tobacco produced on excess acreage. In 1936, 24 percent of the base acreage was diverted, while in 1937, 19 percent was diverted. Harvested acreage in 1936 was slightly below that of 1935. Yields were down, however, and while the price was 10 percent above 1935, total receipts fell. In view of the favorable 1936 price, harvested acreage increased in 1937, while the diverted acreage fell. Despite this increase, the price actually rose slightly and total receipts increased.

The soil conservation program was not proving to be an effective supply control program for most crops, so Congress in February 1938 passed a second Agricultural Adjustment Act. This act established marketing quotas for various products with penalties imposed for growers who exceeded them. Before the administrative machinery of the AAA could allocate individual farm quotas, the 1938 crop was in the ground. This was unfortunate, since there was much overplanting and marketing above quota. Growers of such excess tobacco were penalized at 50 percent of the market price. Naturally, there was some unhappiness with the program. Total production was down from 1937, however, and the price stayed approximately the same, so gross receipts were down.

When marketing quotas were announced for the 1939 crop, less than the required two thirds of the growers approved of the proposed quotas in the December 1938 referendum. That vote meant that there was no quota in effect for tobacco in 1939. Harvested acreage increased dramatically. For instance, flue-cured acreage was larger in that year than any year before or since. The market price plummeted, as would be expected. In the midst of the flue-cured auction season in September 1939, war broke out in Europe. Britain, which was our largest single foreign buyer, stopped all purchase of flue-cured tobacco because of a feared foreign exchange problem. Almost 10 percent of potential sales had been removed from the market. In the face of this event and the low prices the markets were closed.

Ultimately the Commodity Credit Corporation (CCC) worked out an agreement among British and U.S. firms. The CCC was to purchase the tobacco for later resale to Britain. Domestic firms would process and store the tobacco. This meant that effectively Britain was at least in the market, and the market reopened. The market price was up from where it had been before the market closed, but the season average price was a third less than it had been in 1938. Not surprisingly, the growers approved a quota for the 1940 crop.

Quotas were in effect in 1940 and throughout the war years. One change, introduced in 1940, continued until the 1960s was that marketing quotas were converted to acreage allotments, so that each grower had an acreage allotment and not a marketing quota. Prices rose in 1940 and again in 1941. In some of the war years there were price controls on tobacco so that prices could not go up. Although quotas on most other commodities were removed as production of food and fiber crops was encouraged, tobacco was deemed not as essential to the war effort, and its quotas were retained throughout the war years. Tobacco, then, came out of the war with a program in place that had been functioning in essentially the same way for six years.

Operation of the Program

In the first few years of the program the Commodity Credit Corporation, a Federal government agency, was responsible for its operation. The CCC funded the purchase of tobacco as well as other products. After 1938 the CCC acquired commodities via nonrecourse loans. If a pile of tobacco did not bring the support price, for example, it went under loan. This direct link with the CCC was severed in 1941 for burley, and 1946 for flue-cured. The Burley Tobacco Growers Association and the Flue-Cured Tobacco Cooperative Stabilization Corporation were (and are) farmer cooperatives designed to handle both the physical and financial requirements of acquiring leaf going under loan. The coops borrowed money from the Commodity Credit Corporation to fund the loans to the farmer. The coops then processed and stored the tobacco. If such tobacco could later be sold at the acquisition price plus storage cost, it was; the CCC loans were repaid, and the growers were paid any excess receipts. In this sense, tobacco representatives and politicians could claim that tobacco production was not being subsidized. Production was restricted, and when tobacco was acquired by the coop it was typically resold later; hence there was no direct government payment to tobacco producers. These observations are not quite accurate, however. The stabilization coops were funded by loans from the Commodity Credit Corporation, which were usually at less than market rates of interest, so there was a direct government cost—albeit a small one—in the total agricultural picture. Also, the U.S. Department of Agriculture provided grading services at no fee.

The quality of tobacco, in both flue-cured and burley, varies by the position of the leaf on the stalk, color, and other characteristics. In speaking of the price for tobacco, one is really talking about an average price, where there is a distribution of prices over a set of grades. Flue-cured grades are shown in Table 3.2. Growers sort their tobacco before bringing it to the warehouse to try to get uniformity of quality in each pile. Some sorting is done more or less automati-

TABLE 3.2
Summary of Standard Flue-Cured Tobacco Grades[a]

Key to Standard Grademarks for Flue-Cured Tobacco

Groups	Qualities	Color Symbols		Combination Symbols	
A – Wrappers	1 – Choice	L – Lemon	V – Greenish	XL – Lug side	
B – Leaf	2 – Fine	F – Orange	GR – Green red	PO – Oxidized primings	
H – Smoking Leaf	3 – Good	FR – Orange red	GK – Green variegated	XO – Oxidized lugs or cutters	
C – Cutters	4 – Fair	R – Red	GG – Gray green		
X – Lugs	5 – Low	K – Variegated	KL – Variegated lemon	BO – Oxidized leaf	
P – Primings	6 – Poor	KR – Variegated red or scorched	KF – Variegated orange	GL – Thin-bodied nondescript	
M – Mixed			KV – Variegated greenish	GF – Medium-bodied non-descript	
N – Nondescript		G – Green	KM – Variegated mixed		

Special factor
W – Wet
U – Unsound
Sand or dirt[b]

Special symbol
S – Slick

Individual Flue-cured Grades

2 Grades of wrappers	Leaf, cont.	Leaf, cont.	Leaf, cont.	Leaf, cont.
A1L	B3F	B3K	B5S	B3KM
A1F	B4F	B4K	B3KL	B4KM
	B5F	B5K	B4KL	B5KM
56 Grades of leaf	B6F	B6K	B5KL	B6KM
B1L	B1FR	B3KR	B6KL	B4G
B2L	B2FR	B4KR	B3KF	B5G
B3L	B3FR	B5KR	B4KF	B6G
B4L	B4FR	B3V	B5KF	B5GR
B5L	B5FR	B4V	B6KF	B4GK
B6L	B6FR	B5V	B4KV	B5GK
B1F	B4R	B3S	B5KV	B6GK
B2F	B5R	B4S	B6KV	B5GG

TABLE 3.2
(Continued)

Individual Flue-cured Grades (Continued)

15 Grades of smoking leaf	17 Grades of cutters, cont.	Lugs, cont.	Lugs, cont.	Mixed, cont.
H3L	C3L	X3L	X4G	M4KM
H4L	C4L	X4L	X5G	M5KM
H5L	C5L	X5L		M4GK
H6L	C1F	X1F	*10 Grades of primings*	M5GK
H1F	C2F	X2F	P2L	
H2F	C3F	X3F	P3L	*13 Grades of nondescript*
H3F	C4F	X4F	P4L	N1L
H4F	C5F	X5F	P5L	N1KL
H6F	C4KR	X3KR	P2F	N1K
H4FR	C4V	X4KR	P3F	N1R
H5FR	C4S	X3C	P4F	N1GL
H6FR	C4KL	X4V	P5F	N1GF
H4K	C4KM	X3S	P4G	N1KV
H5K	C4G	X4KL	P5G	N1GR
H6K	C4GK	X4FK		N1GG
		X4KV	*7 Grades of mixed*	N1PO
17 Grades of cutters	*23 Grades of lugs*		M4F	N1XO
C1L	X1L	X3KM	M5F	N1BO
C2L	X2L	X4KM	M4KR	N2
		X4GK		

[a]Tobacco not covered by the standard grades is designated "NO-G" or "NOG-F."
[b]Special factors "sand" or "dirt" may be applied to all priming grades and to first quality nondescript from the priming side.
Source: U.S. Department of Agriculture Tobacco Market Review, Flue-cured, 1981 Crop. USDA, AMS, April 1982.

cally for flue-cured tobacco, which is harvested leaf by leaf, a process known as "priming" in some areas. The bottom leaves mature first, are picked, and then cured. A grower can be selling some leaves as more leaves are still on the plant in the field. In burley production, the plant is cut down whole and then air-cured. The leaves are then separated from the plant after which the sorting takes place.

Until 1982, the program worked as follows: Growers have agreed in referenda to have a quota program. Individual allotments (pounds and/or acreage) for each farm have been set. Each year the secretary of agriculture has determined the overall quota consistent with the overall support price, which is established by formula. This overall quota takes into account stocks held by the stabilization corporations, demand conditions, and other factors that might affect the market. (Changes in the support price formula will be discussed shortly, when pressures on the program are described.) Originally, under the Agricultural Act of 1949, the support price was to be a price that was 90 percent of parity, where the parity price was based on the preceding 10 years' average price.

This mandated price is the average support price for the whole crop. How is this translated into a price that would apply to an individual pile of tobacco? This is where the grading system comes in. The distribution of grades is estimated based on previous crops. Each grade is then given a support price, so that the distribution of these prices, weighted by the proportion of tobacco in each grade, will yield the overall average support price. Table 3.3 shows the distribution by grades of the support for flue-cured tobacco prices for 1981. Clearly, the grade given to his tobacco is of vital importance to the grower, since he is guaranteed the price of the grade for that pile.

Each pile of tobacco placed on the floor is given a grade by a government grader. These graders are federal government employees, and are therefore independent of buyers, growers, or warehouse owners. The grade is written on a tag, and the auctioneer and the buyers know the support price associated with each grade. The auction takes place with the auctioneer and the buyers walking along a row of piles of tobacco. At each pile the auctioneer starts the bidding at or above the support price for the grade displayed. If the result of the auction is a price higher than the support price, the tobacco goes to the highest bidder. If no bid is received above the

TABLE 3.3
Season Average Prices Per 100 Pounds of Tobacco by Types in the Flue-Cured Area and Schedule of Loan Rates, 1981 Crop

Group and Grade	1981 Crop Season Averages Type 11–14 (dollars)[a]	1981 Loan Rate Type 11–14 (dollars)
Wrappers		
A1L	—	203
A1F	—	203
Leaf		
B1L	194	193
B2L	192	189
B3L	189	186
B4L	188	182
B5L	182	174
B6L	174	168
B1F	194	193
B2F	191	189
B3F	190	186
B4F	188	182
B5F	183	174
B6F	176	168
B1FR	—	191
B2FR	—	187
B3FR	188	184
B4FR	186	181
B5FR	179	173
B6FR	(168)	166
B4R	—	160
B5R	166	152
B3K	183	178
B4K	179	172
B5K	172	165
B6K	163	157
B3KR	182	175
B4KR	179	171
B5KR	171	162
B3V	184	174
B4V	181	169

TABLE 3.3
(Continued)

Group and Grade	1981 Crop Season Averages Type 11–14 (dollars)[a]	1981 Loan Rate Type 11–14 (dollars)
Leaf (Continued)		
B5V	174	160
B3S	181	166
B4S	178	162
B5S	169	156
B3KL	178	165
B4KL	173	161
B5KL	167	155
B6KL	156	146
B3KF	175	165
B4KF	170	161
B5KF	164	155
B6KF	155	146
B4KV	170	158
B5KV	162	148
B6KV	153	138
B3KM	181	169
B4KM	177	165
B5KM	171	159
B6KM	163	148
B4G	168	151
B5G	161	145
B6G	149	133
B5GR	150	133
B4GK	165	146
B5GK	158	142
B6GK	150	133
B5GG	146	118
Smoking leaf		
H3L	190	188
H4L	188	185
H5L	185	177
H6L	—	172
H1F	—	195

TABLE 3.3
(Continued)

Group and Grade	1981 Crop Season Averages Type 11–14 (dollars)[a]	1981 Loan Rate Type 11–14 (dollars)
Smoking leaf (Continued)		
H2F	(192)	191
H3F	190	188
H4F	189	185
H5F	185	177
H6F	(183)	172
H4FR	—	181
H5FR	180	174
H6FR	(169)	167
H4K	182	171
H5K	178	166
H6K	169	158
Cutters		
C1L	195	195
C2L	194	192
C3L	190	189
C4L	187	185
C5L	181	177
C1F	—	195
C2F	193	192
C3F	190	189
C4F	187	185
C5F	182	177
C4KR	180	172
C4V	179	171
C4S	177	167
C4KL	174	163
C4KM	177	166
C4G	168	154
C4GK	167	148
Lugs		
X1L	(190)	190
X2L	186	184

TABLE 3.3
(Continued)

Group and Grade	1981 Crop Season Averages Type 11–14 (dollars)[a]	1981 Loan Rate Type 11–14 (dollars)
Lugs (Continued)		
X3L	179	177
X4L	172	166
X5L	159	150
X1F	190	190
X2F	186	184
X3F	181	177
X4F	174	166
X5F	161	150
X3KR	176	166
X4KR	171	160
X3V	174	165
X4V	168	159
X3S	172	160
X4KL	162	147
X4KF	161	147
X4KV	156	143
X3KM	173	157
X4KM	166	150
X4GK	157	139
X4G	157	145
X5G	148	139
Primings		
P2L	169	136
P2L sand	—	122
P3L	160	128
P3L sand	142	115
P4L	150	117
P4L sand	138	105
P5L	136	—
P5L sand	121	—
P2F	171	136
P2F sand	169	122
P3F	160	128

TABLE 3.3
(Continued)

Group and Grade	1981 Crop Season Averages Type 11–14 (dollars)[a]	1981 Loan Rate Type 11–14 (dollars)
Primings (Continued)		
P3F sand	147	115
P4F	148	117
P4F sand	134	105
P5F	133	—
P5F sand	122	—
P4G	143	107
P4G sand	135	96
P5G	131	—
P5G sand	121	—
Mixed		
M4F	—	147
M5F	164	144
M4KR	—	138
M4KM	161	135
M5KM	157	130
M4GK	(157)	132
M5GK	147	124
Nondescript		
N1L	122	—
N1L sand	111	—
N1XL	134	—
N1K	145	120
N1R	135	110
N1GL	126	—
N1GL sand	111	—
N1GF	137	110
N1KV	140	109
N1GR	138	104
N1GG	131	101
N1PO	129	—
N1PO sand	125	—
N1XO	142	—

TABLE 3.3
(Continued)

Group and Grade	1981 Crop Season Averages Type 11–14 (dollars)[a]	1981 Loan Rate Type 11–14 (dollars)
Nondescript (Continued)		
N1BO	152	102
N2	115	—
NOG	120	—
NOG-F sand	127	—
"W"	130	—
"U"	129	—

[a]In column 2, dashes indicate less than 10 lots sold; parentheses indicate between 10 and 20 lots sold.

Source: U.S. Department of Agriculture. 1982.

support price, three things can happen. Most likely, the tobacco will go to the stabilization corporation. The buyer can refuse the sale, however, and try to sell it later. Finally, the warehouse can buy it at or above the support price and try to resell it later.

The amount of tobacco that goes to the stabilization corporation thus depends on demand and supply conditions at the time of the auction, as well as the distribution of grades. Since tobacco is storable in processed form, tobacco companies can postpone buying, depending on conditions at the time and those predicted for the future. Some grades may be in excess supply at the support price. The larger the amount going under loan, the more pressure there is on the program. Since the price is set by law, the operational variable to adjust is quota. As we will now see, the pressure on the program forced the first major change in the program in 1965.

1946–65

The period 1946–65 was one of relative stability in the price support program, interspersed with periods of severe pressure on the program. Until 1965 the pressures were alleviated by changing allotment size, and by various technical adjustments to the program. As can be seen in Tables 3.4 and 3.5, years that saw a large quantity of tobacco going under loan were followed typically by reductions in

TABLE 3.4
Number of Allotments and Acreage or Poundage 1959–82

Year	Flue-Cured		Burley	
	Allotments (number)	Acreage (acres)	Allotments (number)	Acreage (acres)
1959	207,331	712,558	302,805	309,140
1960	205,331	713,313	302,307	309,376
1961	202,737	714,203	300,623	328,600
1962	201,741	745,238	301,142	348,572
1963	201,198	708,489	299,843	348,910
1964	198,075	638,240	298,633	315,698
1965	192,662	606,648	295,416	286,601
1966	192,413	606,665	292,537	249,944
1967	194,475	607,316	288,086	249,926
1968	194,378	607,786	284,752	249,966
1969	194,381	607,869	282,875	249,761
1970	193,925	577,723	282,115	230,947
				1,000 lbs.
1971	192,771	577,735	285,731	555,063
1972	192,067	577,737	288,634	531,466
1973	191,588	635,745	291,738	559,723
		1,000 lbs.		
1974	191,291	1,337,117	294,687	607,828
1975	192,045	1,572,021	296,882	750,441
1976	192,610	1,409,078	295,516	726,354
1977	192,552	1,197,274	298,107	683,434
1978	193,094	1,181,459	300,284	667,789
1979	192,759	1,070,245	303,186	647,765
1980	194,195	1,186,493	304,109	768,910
1981	195,179	1,111,414	305,972	841,915
1982	195,029	978,433	309,046	783,774

Source: U.S. Department of Agriculture. Various years. *Annual Report of Tobacco Statistics.*

acreage. In the crop years 1955 and 1956 more than 20 percent of the flue-cured crop wound up in stabilization stocks, and severe pressure was being put on the program.

TABLE 3.5
Flue-Cured and Burley Tobacco Going Under Loan

Year	Flue-Cured (1,000 lb)	Percentage of Crop	Burley (1,000 lb)	Percentage of Crop
1955	298,867	20.2	73,054	15.5
1956	319,879	22.5	6,045	1.2
1957	107,807	11.1	16,639	3.4
1958	144,845	13.4	11,204	2.4
1959	55,296	5.1	13,216	2.6
1960	51,761	4.1	8,417	1.7
1961	70,317	5.6	10,272	1.8
1962	237,036	16.8	63,517	9.4
1963	277,165	20.2	202,312	26.8
1964	285,582	20.7	110,431	17.9
1965	71,493	6.8	42,228	7.2
1966	74,574	6.7	62,534	10.7
1967	282,077	22.6	64,168	11.9
1968	128,779	12.9	56,192	10.0
1969	97,587	9.3	158,540	26.7
1970	144,226	12.2	47,660	8.6
1971	55,670	5.1	178	—
1972	24,281	2.3	22,837	3.9
1973	30,778	2.7	660	.1
1974	22,988	1.9	2,547	.4
1975	259,029	18.4	51,194	8.0
1976	276,902	21.1	46,185	7.1
1977	193,085	17.2	57,054	9.3
1978	63,591	5.3	67,590	11.4
1979	69,824	7.4	7,162	1.6
1980	137,229	12.6	21	—
1981	105,863	9.3	802	.1
1982	259,900	26.3	268,400	34.7

Source: U.S. Department of Agriculture. Various years. *Annual Report of Tobacco Statistics.*

This accumulation was the direct result of the support program itself. Since the variable being controlled is acreage, each individual farmer has an incentive to produce as many pounds as he can. Quantity of production is stimulated rather than quality, or any other attribute of tobacco. It is not surprising that yield per acre had a marked upward trend throughout the period of acreage controls, allowing for year-to-year weather fluctuations. In the years shortly preceding the 1955 crop three new varieties of flue-cured tobacco had been introduced. These varieties were high yielding and easy to grow and cure, and therefore popular with farmers. Unfortunately, they had some characteristics that buyers did not like: They were light bodied, pale, and low in nicotine. To further compound the mismatching of supply and demand, the switch to filter tip cigarettes was just under way, and precisely the opposite set of characteristics was in demand. Another feature of the new varieties was that their characteristics distorted the distribution of grades, so that the weights used to set the prices on individual grades were at variance with those used for the recent past. As a consequence of all these factors, a large fraction of the 1955 and 1956 crops went under loan.

The remedy for the problem was to reduce the support price of the suspect varieties to 50 percent of the regular support price for tobacco. This was done in 1957, effectively stopping the production of those varieties. The program was able to continue as before.

Two laws passed in the 1950s that affected tobacco were Public Law 480, passed in 1954, and the Soil Bank Act of 1956. The former was the food assistance act that called for the sale in foreign currency and some donations of U.S. agricultural products to less developed countries. Tobacco was included in the group of commodities eligible for such exports. Such exports have not been very large in terms of percentage of total sales, but they do add at the margin to the total demand for tobacco.

The Soil Bank program was designed to take land out of production for conservation purposes. Tobacco came under the legislation. Again, the acreage of tobacco removed was not very great, but at the margin there was some price effect from slightly lower production.

In 1960 Congress passed legislation to change the method of price supports. The new support levels would be based on a three year moving average of the Parity Index. This action was designed to slow the rate of increase in the price of tobacco.

The next substantive change in the program came in 1961, when legislation was passed that permitted flue-cured allotment to be leased and transferred from the farm to which the allotment had originally been granted. Previously the only way a grower could acquire tobacco allotment was to buy a farm with an allotment in place. Historically, flue-cured tobacco had been grown on larger scale operations than burley; the larger units for flue-cured were typically share cropping operations. As allotments were being scaled back to maintain the support price, some allotments became uneconomical and larger units could not expand. Also, by 1961 the original allotments granted in 1933 were almost 30 years old. Retaining interest in property but not growing tobacco, was a restrictive option. The lease and transfer option itself was restricted to within counties: allotments could not be moved from low-yielding counties to higher-yielding ones. Even so, yields continued to rise, stabilization stocks increased, and pressure on the program continued. Resource use was distorted. Table 3.1, in the first part of this chapter, shows a loss due to inefficiencies. This loss refers to the resource distortion that comes from restraining output by restricting only one input—land. The combination of resources used to grow tobacco moved further and further from the optimum.

In 1965, this large inefficiency loss was largely reduced for flue-cured tobacco when a change was made in setting of allotments. The system was changed from an acreage allotment to an acreage–poundage program. A grower received both an acreage and poundage quota based on the individual's production history. As the program evolved, this became essentially a poundage program, as the pounds marketed became the binding constraint. This change in the program did not take all the pressure off the program, but it did alleviate it somewhat.

Accompanying the switch from acreage controls to poundage controls was a new allowance for good and bad years. The pounds produced depends not only on acreage, but on yield, which, in turn, is related to weather and other phenomena. Therefore, the grower is allowed to sell 10 percent more than his quota in any given year, with the proviso that he sell 10 percent less the following year. For the reverse case, where the farmer's yield is less than anticipated, he can sell more the next year. In this case an unlimited amount of quota can be carried over. Output of both burley and flue-cured tobacco is greatly stabilized in this fashion.

1965–82

The program continued largely unaltered from 1965 to 1982. In 1971 the burley program was changed to an acreage–poundage program, and there were some changes in the marketing requirements: Tying into hands (see Chapter 5) was no longer required for flue-cured, and some experimental marketings of baled burley tobacco were allowed. Little else was changed. The program stayed under pressure, however, as the use of tobacco in cigarettes was assailed for health reasons. The details of this health issue are described in Chapter 4. Another pressure, especially for flue-cured, came from the export market. The support price formula caused the price to remain above the world price, and U.S. tobacco became overpriced when compared to alternative sources. The U.S. share of the market fell, even though the physical volume of U.S. exports stayed about the same. This pressure was attenuated for several years by events abroad.

In 1967 Rhodesia declared herself independent of Great Britain. This led to United Nations sanctions against Rhodesia, including an embargo on Rhodesian exports. Rhodesia had been our closest competitor both in terms of volume and quality. Its market share had been increasing at the same time the U.S. share had been falling. Therefore, the Rhodesian embargo pushed our chief competitor in the international flue-cured market back down their supply curve. It is fairly evident, although no data exist, that some tobacco continued to be exported from Rhodesia. In any event, the trend in U.S. market share was changed, as other competitors did not fill in the whole Rhodesian shortfall until later in the 1970s. Rhodesia was renamed Zimbabwe under a new government, and its current exports are recorded. As of 1982 they had not regained their former position, but they are expected to do so.

A second reason U.S. exports did not actually decline from the increased prices was the income effect. Tobacco has a positive income elasticity, and real income was rising in the rest of the world. Despite these favorable developments, pressure on the program continued to mount.

Pressure on the burley program was less than that on flue-cured. One reason, as mentioned, was that less burley is exported, and there is consequently less pressure from world markets. In addition, a quality problem had arisen in flue-cured tobacco. With the lease and transfer program large units for growing tobacco became feasible. Labor costs were rising and mechanization of both curing and harvesting operations was on the rise. Mechanization itself affected to some extent the physical characteristics of tobacco; however it had another effect: With large units using relatively little labor, the grade price differential offered the grower less incentive to handle his tobacco in such a way as to get the highest grade possible. Some foreign buyers who had always considered U.S. tobacco to be a uniform, high quality tobacco expressed concern (Campbell 1981).

Several schemes were tried to alleviate the pressure. At one point growers were to be rewarded with extra acreage allotment if they did not harvest the lowest leaves. In 1980 the support price was lowered directly for the eight lowest quality grades. These efforts helped somewhat, but did not totally solve the problem. The next significant change in the program came in 1982.

The "no net cost" tobacco program of 1982 has some features that are not related to the buildup of stocks and the foreign demand issue. A checkoff was established whereby growers would be assessed the cost of the grading service. It was also to cover the expenses of the stabilization coop, which had previously been done with loans from the CCC (to be repaid from sale proceeds). Another feature was that allotments could be sold separately from the land. In fact, such sales were mandated for quotas held by nonfarm interests, such as utilities, that had acquired quotas in land purchases.

The feature of the program that should affect the demand side is the authority given to the secretary of agriculture to affect the support price. He was empowered to put into place only 65 percent of the increase in the support price that would be required by the parity formula. The secretary did this for the 1982 crop, but, for whatever reasons, a relatively large quantity of that crop went under loan. At the time of writing, tobacco growers in the flue-cured area are fractionalized over rental rates for allotments and sale prices of allotments. They are also disgruntled over the costs of the program.

Overall Assessment of the Program

Tobacco is unique among U.S. agricultural products in that it was produced under essentially the same price support program from World War II to 1982. Most other products that have had price support programs have seen sharp changes in those programs, and for some years have experienced no programs at all. Are there any conclusions about the tobacco program that can be reached in an objective fashion?

One result of the tobacco program was to remove almost all price variations from flue-cured and burley tobacco. Table 3.6 gives nominal price and support figures for tobacco, which are then converted in Table 3.7 to constant dollar prices. All prices are in 1967 dollars, using the Consumer Price Index, where 1967 equals 100. A glance at Table 3.7 shows how remarkably stable these prices are. Flue-cured ranges from 54.9 to 74.8 cents per pound, but only 6 out of 29 observations are not in the 60–69 cents-per-pound range. For burley the range is slightly wider—53.2 to 77 cents per pound—but the mean price is also slightly higher. Thus there are 6 more observations in the 70–79 cents-per-pound range.

This remarkable stability is highlighted when compared with another agricultural commodity—wheat. Table 3.8 presents some measures concerning two time series of postwar prices—the prices of flue-cured tobacco and hard red winter wheat, for the 1947–76 time period. All prices are expressed as real prices in 1967 dollars. Tobacco, of course, has had a relatively consistent program, while wheat had a variety of price support programs during this period. In fact, during parts of the period there was no support program for wheat. For most of this period the real price of wheat had a pronounced downward trend. For tobacco the price range is from 61.6 to 75.9 cents per pound. For hard red winter wheat the range in price

TABLE 3.6
Average Price Received by Farmers and Average Support Price for Flue-Cured and Burley Tobacco (cents per pound)

Year	Flue-Cured		Burley	
	Avg. Price Received	Avg. Support Price	Avg. Price Received	Avg. Support Price
1934–38	22.9	—	22.2	—
1939–43	27.6	—	30.0	—
1944–48	45.0	—	43.5	—
1949–53	51.5	—	49.6	—
1954–58	54.1	—	59.7	—
1957	55.4	50.8	60.3	51.7
1958	58.2	54.6	66.1	55.4
1959	58.3	55.5	60.6	57.2
1960	60.4	55.5	64.3	57.2
1961	64.3	55.5	66.5	57.2
1962	60.1	56.1	58.6	57.8
1963	58.0	56.6	59.2	58.3
1964	58.5	57.2	60.3	58.9
1965	64.6	57.7	67.0	59.5
1966	66.9	58.8	66.9	60.6
1967	64.9	59.9	71.8	61.8
1968	65.6	61.6	73.7	63.5
1969	72.4	63.8	69.6	65.8
1970	72.0	66.6	72.2	68.6
1971	77.2	69.4	80.9	71.5
1972	85.3	72.2	79.2	74.9
1973	88.1	76.6	92.9	78.9
1974	105.1	83.3	113.8	83.8
1975	99.8	93.2	105.5	96.1
1976	110.4	106.0	114.2	109.3
1977	117.6	113.8	120.0	117.3
1978	135.0	121.0	131.0	124.7
1979	140.0	129.3	145.2	133.3
1980	144.5	141.5	165.9	145.9

Source: U.S. Department of Agriculture. Various years. *Annual Report of Tobacco Statistics.*

TABLE 3.7
**Real Prices for Flue-Cured and Burley Tobacco in Constant
1967 Dollars**

Year	Flue-Cured (cents per pound)	Burley (cents per pound)
1934–38	54.9	53.2
1939–43	60.4	65.6
1944–48	73.9	71.4
1949–53	67.6	55.1
1954–56	65.5	72.3
1957	65.7	74.1
1958	67.2	74.1
1959	70.2	69.4
1960	68.1	72.5
1961	74.8	74.2
1962	66.3	64.7
1963	63.2	64.6
1964	63.0	64.9
1965	68.4	70.9
1966	68.8	68.8
1967	64.9	71.8
1968	63.0	70.8
1969	65.9	63.4
1970	61.9	62.1
1971	63.6	66.7
1972	68.1	63.2
1973	66.2	69.8
1974	71.2	77.0
1975	61.9	65.4
1976	64.8	67.0
1977	64.8	66.1
1978	69.1	67.0
1979	64.4	66.8
1980	58.5	67.2

Source: Compiled by the author

is from $1.27 to $3.89 per bushel. The mean price and the standard error for each series is also shown. The summary statistic that shows the relative variability of the two series is the coefficient of variation,

TABLE 3.8
A Comparison of Price Stability for Flue-Cured Tobacco and Hard Red Winter Wheat, 1947–76 (in constant 1967 dollars)

	Tobacco	*Wheat*
Lowest price	61.6 cents/lb.	$1.27/bushel
Highest price	75.9 cents/lb.	$3.89/bushel
Mean price	66.3 cents/lb.	$2.32/bushel
Standard deviation	3.499	.865
Coefficient of variation	5.27%	37.28%

Source: Compiled by the author.

which is the standard deviation divided by the mean. This measure can be expressed as a percentage. For flue-cured tobacco the standard deviation is 5.27 percent, while for wheat it is 37.28 percent. This difference is quite striking. Whatever one thinks of the supply control program, price uncertainty has certainly been removed for tobacco growers.

As noted earlier, the support program greatly stabilizes output as well. Tobacco growers, then, have seen both price and output uncertainty removed from their decisionmaking process. In recent years growing tobacco has been as close to a sure thing as one can find in U.S. agriculture.

The original AAA legislation and subsequent legislation was designed to transfer income from consumers and/or taxpayers to producers of certain commodities. Since these transfers were to be effected through the marketplace they have both political and economic effects. I originally thought that this study of tobacco could serve as a study of support programs in general. Tobacco, as a regionally concentrated commodity that is quite small in terms of gross receipts, would be a microcosm for the larger world of agricultural commodities. I have reservations now about that view. For one thing, tobacco supports never represented the drain on the treasury that, for example, milk supports did and do. If it had not been for the health issue, the tobacco program would probably have been barely noticed, except as another case of intervention in the market. A consequence of this low treasury cost is that changes in the program that have occurred since the war can be viewed as endogenous. Growers voted overwhelmingly in referenda to keep the program. When problems arose in the operation of the program, changes were made at its margin. Acreage-poundage and lease and transfer were changes in the program, but they were not fundamental in nature. They were changes in response to problems specific to tobacco. Such was not the case for the major commodities such as wheat, feed grains, and cotton during the 1950s, 1960s, and 1970s. Fairly substantial changes in programs for these commodities took place throughout the period.

Another reason that the tobacco program cannot be considered a microcosm is that U.S. monopoly power in the worldwide production of tobacco has been greater than that for most major crops. Even in soybeans (which does not have a support program) where the U.S. market share is very large, there is not much monopoly power. The reason, of course, is that there are substitute crops that yield the same end products. As was shown earlier, this monopoly power generates national income to the United States. This was an unintended result of a politically engendered income transfer program, but it exists nevertheless. The usual demonstrations of lost producer and consumer surplus are offset by revenue gains.

A third interesting difference for the tobacco program involves the health issue. The program is an income transfer program, whereby income is transferred from consumers to producers. Tobacco consumers are the ones who are at potential risk from the effects of smoking. Two side effects are brought about by raising the price of the program: First, consumption is reduced and there is less smoking. Second, by paying the higher price the smokers are paying for the transfer to producers, in effect taxing themselves. These bits of irony seem lost on certain antismoking individuals and groups.

Appendix

The use of consumers and producers surplus concepts has been subject to attack practically since Alfred Marshall reintroduced the concepts originated by Depuit. One seeks, in analyses such as that in this book, a measure of the money value of consumers' utility and producers' opportunity costs. Harberger (1971) adds a third condition, asserting that distributional effects can be ignored. This last assertion, the third of Harberger's "Three Postulates," does not present any serious problem for the current measurement. Therefore it is not considered. Since most of the controversy surrounds the consumers surplus issue, an attempt will be made first to clarify the supply curve as a measure of opportunity cost.

If we assume competitive markets, then no one seems to object to the concept that the competitive supply price for a unit measures the value of that unit to the suppliers. Producers surplus, then, measures the area under the competitive price and to the left of the supply curve. This represents the value of resources that would be needed if the same price were paid for all units. Mishan (1968) has objected to this usage, and prefers to call these rents. This problem seems to be semantic, and nothing further need be said about it.

Controversy continues over the use of consumer surplus as a dollar measure of utility, however. If we are going to measure losses as we move away from a competitive equilibrium, it is necessary that the measure chosen does in fact accomplish that objective. Harberger (1971) gives an eloquent plea for the use of consumer surplus in welfare calculations. Silberberg (1978) argues strongly against this position. The issue is whether consumers surplus is a good approximation, or, as Silberberg and McKenzie and Pearce (1982) argue, an approximation at all, of an exact measure of a change in utility from a price change. There appears to be agreement on several points. First, the exact measure sought is one of the Hicksian measures of compensating or equivalent variation. Second, there are potential problems when more than one good is involved. Technically, what is at issue in the latter case is the path independence of the welfare indicator. Also, there seems to be agreement that for a partial equilibrium analysis, consumers surplus, for a normal good, will lie between the two Hicksian measures.

The Willig (1976) treatment of the issue applies directly to the one market equilibrium to which the use of consumers surplus seems fully justified. In fact, it is difficult to see any other course. We observe market transactions and market demand curves. In general, we do not observe real income constant demand curves, and the Hicksian measures are not available. Since this is an empirical problem, the measures used here will have to suffice.

4

CHANGES IN DEMAND AND HEALTH ISSUES

The year 1964 represents a watershed for the cigarette industry. In that year the Federal Government took a negative position on the smoking and health issue. The surgeon general of the United States issued a report entitled *Smoking and Health,* which presented a statistical study linking smoking and decreased longevity. This last term is used advisedly, since the evidence seems to indicate that cigarette smokers die younger of many diseases than do nonsmokers. The major focus of the work, however, was on an increased incidence of lung cancer. For the first time, an agency of the Federal Government officially endorsed the view that cigarette smoking was dangerous in any way.

Antitobacco sentiment goes back as far as James I of England, who wrote a tract, "Counterblaste to Tobacco," in 1604, before tobacco was grown by the colonists in Jamestown (Robert 1967). In those days, tobacco was consumed as snuff or in pipes. There was a very vocal antitobacco group in the nineteenth century that died out with the Civil War. During this period, chewing tobacco was the leading item in the U.S. method of consumption. With the introduction of the cigarette making machine, cigarette smoking increased rapidly in the United States. From the turn of the century to the 1930s, increased consumption was accompanied by great activity of the antismokers. Some of this activity was loosely connected to the Prohibition movement. Much exaggeration was produced on both sides of the issue. Neither medical science nor the field of statistics was sufficiently advanced to produce either clinical or epidemiological evidence of a link between smoking and any particular disease.

After World War II, medical and public health research became much more sophisticated. Studies during the 1950s tended more and more to find a putative statistical connection between tobacco and lung and cardiovascular diseases. These studies culminated in a report by the British Government in 1962, and the celebrated 1964 report in the United States. Both indicted cigarette smoking as a factor in the incidence of serious diseases.

As expected, organizations associated with tobacco, such as the Tobacco Institute, reacted negatively to the report. Since the study presented an essentially statistical case against tobacco, independent statisticians also reviewed the report. In certain areas the study was found deficient in statistical methods and inferences. As recently as 1979, the Tobacco Institute produced a report, "Smoking and Health 1964–1979, the Continuing Controversy," attempting to refute many of the findings of the Surgeon General's report. In the same year the Department of Health, Education and Welfare updated the 1964 report. The new report was even tougher on smoking than the original. The scientific controversy has not been completely resolved, but certainly the public thinks it has been, and this has had and will have an effect on the markets for tobacco products. No stand is to be taken here on whether smoking is good, bad, or neutral. Rather, the impact on the economics of tobacco is what is to be examined.

The 1964 report led to the introduction of smoking as a public policy issue. The antitobacco forces clearly gained the advantage, as the following chronology of legislative and administrative actions following 1964 attests (see also Pugh 1981).

1964   The Federal Trade Commission issues a trade regulation requiring a health warning on cigarette packages and in cigarette advertising.

1965   PL 89–82, the Federal Cigarette Labeling and Advertising Act of 1965, requiring a health warning on cigarette packages, takes effect.

1967   The Federal Communications commission requires that broadcast stations carrying cigarette advertising must also carry a significant amount of antismoking messages.

1968   The FTC recommends that Congress ban television and radio cigarette advertising.

1970   PL 91–222, The Public Health Cigarette Smoking Act of 1970 is signed into law, prohibiting advertising of cigarettes on radio and television and strengthening the warning label on cigarette packs.

1970   The FTC issues a proposed ruling requiring the disclosure of tar and nicotine content of cigarettes in advertising. The proposal is suspended when manufacturers offer voluntarily to make the disclosures.

1973   The Civil Aeronautics Board approves a regulation requiring that domestic airlines designate "no smoking" areas aboard aircraft.

1978   HEW Secretary Califano announces new government initiatives to combat smoking, including the formation of a new office on smoking and health.

1979   The General Services Administration establishes smoking rules on a governmentwide basis.

Obviously, all of these regulations are designed to lower the consumption of cigarettes. Before looking at that outcome, however, let us consider the advertising ban. Cigarettes are advertised by brand. That is, the ads do not say smoking is good for you; they say that brand X has some superior quality that should cause you to switch to it. The glamour of the ads and their ubiquity may have led some people to smoke who would not otherwise have done so, but several earlier studies of both cigarettes and other industries confirmed that advertising of brands has little or no effect on demand for the product as a whole. Two recent studies of the effect of the cigarette advertising ban shed new light on the role of advertising in cigarette consumption. One, "The Effects of Government Regulation on Teen-Age Smoking" (Lewit, Coate, and Grossman 1981), deals with a subject of great concern because lifetime smoking habits may be initiated in those years. The second, "Government Regulation of Cigarette Health Information" (Schneider, Klein, and Murphy 1981) looks at the broader issue of the effect on tobacco consumption. Before looking at the results of these studies, a bit more information about the setting seems warranted.

As noted in the chronology, in 1967 the Federal Communications Commission required that TV and radio stations carrying cigarette ads must also carry antismoking ads. This edict was an application of the Fairness Doctrine, which holds that both sides of controversial issues should be given an equal opportunity to be heard. The intent was clear: brand advertising would be offset by advertising against all brands. This policy lasted only about three years, and was replaced by the ban on advertising in 1970. Have these policies been effective? There are two economic aspects of this question: One is whether government regulation is effective, and the second concerns the value of information.

An item of some importance to both studies is that cigarette consumption in the United States peaked before either policy was introduced. Lewit, Coate, and Grossman present a table of the percentage of adults by age groups who are regular smokers. In both sexes and for all age groups the percentage fell from 1966 to 1970 and then fell further until 1975. For instance, 59 percent of 35–44 year old males were regular smokers in 1966, but only 48.6 were in 1970, and 47.1 in 1975. Per capita cigarette consumption as reported by the U.S. Department of Agriculture peaked in 1963. These changes in consumption are taken up in the next section, but it should be noted here that they complicate statistical inference from the cigarette data. The two studies under discussion are careful attempts to get around these complications.

Previous studies had concluded that the antismoking ads under the fairness doctrine were not effective. Lewit, Coate, and Grossman, on the other hand, conclude that the antismoking campaign was successful, and had a substantial negative impact on teenage smoking. The study also found that teenage smoking peaked in 1974. The authors do not explain this, but their conjecture is that it is in part a result of the decline in adult smoking. Even though teenage smoking continued to grow from 1970 to 1974, a deterrence effect cannot be ruled out, as the real price of cigarettes was falling at the same time. As Table 7.3 in Chapter 7 shows, the real rate of federal taxes on cigarettes fell as U.S. inflation grew. The postwar rate of 8 cents per pack stayed fixed until 1982. Thus, as inflation occurred, the real price of cigarettes was falling.

The authors also ran a regression analysis of teenage smoking on several variables. The observations were made on a panel of teenagers who were interviewed between 1966 and 1970 by the National Center for Health Statistics. Several interesting results emerged from their analysis. The price elasticity of the demand for cigarettes is much higher for teenagers than for adults. Their estimate is − 1.4 for teenagers as opposed to an elasticity of around − .4 for adults. This finding is significant in that an increase in the federal excise tax, as occurred in 1982, should have a bigger impact on teenage smoking than on adult smoking. It is, of course, too early to try to confirm that finding, and the evidence would be hard to get, but the impact of the tax increase might be greater in the long run than the short run.

The regression analysis is the source of the conclusion on the effect of advertising. They included several measures of antismoking messages. The coefficients on these variables have the expected signs and in general are statistically significant, thus the authors conclude that the Fairness Doctrine had a strong negative impact on teenage smoking.

The Schneider, Klein, and Murphy study is concerned with the more general problem of the impact of all information sources on smoking. Their study is concerned with a 1953 American Cancer Society report and the 1964 Surgeon General's report, as well as the advertising changes. Previous studies had tried to demonstrate that the 1953 and 1964 reports were ineffectual. The study under discussion incorporates the technical changes in cigarettes during the 1950s and 1960s. One of the biggest changes was the increased use of filter tips. This results in use of less tobacco per cigarette, and was clearly related to the health issues. When this fact is taken into account, tobacco consumption per capita (as opposed to cigarette con-

TABLE 4.1
Per Capita Consumption of Cigarettes and Tobacco

| | Per Capita 18 Years and Over | | |
| | Cigarettes | | All Tobacco Products |
Year	(number)	(pounds of tobacco)	(pounds)
1925–29 Avg.	1,285	3.56	9.86
1930–34 Avg.	1,389	3.82	8.80
1935–39 Avg.	1,779	4.81	9.22
1940–44 Avg.	2,558	6.97	10.88
1945–49 Avg.	3,459	9.38	12.46
1950–54 Avg.	3,965	9.98	12.61
1955–59 Avg.	3,806	9.39	11.71
1960	4,171	9.64	11.82
1961	4,266	9.84	12.00
1962	4,265	9.69	11.80
1963	4,345	9.70	11.78
1964	4,194	9.21	11.54
1965	4,258	9.37	11.51
1966	4,287	9.08	11.12
1967	4,280	8.86	10.80
1968	4,186	8.69	10.59
1969	3,993	8.11	10.04
1970	3,985	7.77	9.68
1971	4,042	7.76	9.54
1972	4,047	7.66	9.41
1973	4,147	7.92	9.53
1974	4,141	7.90	9.40
1975	4,121	7.75	9.14
1976	4,092	7.35	8.69
1977	4,051	7.21	8.49
1978	3,967	6.89	8.10
1979	3,850	6.97	8.12
1980	3,845	6.87	7.98
1981	3,840	6.91	8.00

Source: U.S. Department of Agriculture. Annual Reports of Tobacco Statistics.

sumption) peaked in 1953. Table 4.1 shows the trend in cigarette and tobacco consumption. The data clearly reveal that tobacco consumption peaked before cigarette consumption did. Table 4.2 shows

TABLE 4.2
Cigarettes Per Pound of Leaf

Year	Number
1939–43 Avg.	319
1944–48 Avg.	327
1949–53 Avg.	327
1954–58 Avg.	355
1958	380
1959	386
1960	382
1961	388
1962	398
1963	404
1964	404
1965	410
1966	438
1967	428
1968	442
1969	430
1970	467
1971	454
1972	469
1973	471
1974	457
1975	491
1976	494
1977	489
1978	501
1979	489
1980	523

Source: U.S. Department of Agriculture. *Annual Reports of Tobacco Statistics.*

the quite sharp decrease from the 1950s to the 1970s in the amount of tobacco in a cigarette. Tobacco consumption fell, and this fall was intensified by the 1964 report. They conclude that the two effects accounted for a 25 percent drop in consumption from 1953 to 1971. Another 5 percent drop is attributed to the Fairness Doctrine anti-smoking ads, for a total drop of 30 percent. They then conclude that the effect of the advertising ban actually increased smoking. This finding is at variance with earlier findings of a negative effect of the ban. They attribute the difference to the superior specification of their model. This certainly seems plausible in light of the comments above. One should note that tobacco consumption in the United States continues to fall on a per capita basis. The effect was to slow this trend, not to reverse it.

One has to be careful in interpreting the data on cigarette consumption. While per capita consumption of both cigarettes and tobacco has fallen, total U.S. consumption of both has increased over this period. Total U.S. consumption of cigarettes went from 536.5 billion in 1970 to 640 billion in 1981. World production of cigarettes shows a pronounced upward trend through the 1970s also. It is even likely that world per capita consumption of cigarettes continues to increase. World production increased from an average output in 1968–72 of 3,350 billion to 4,561 billion in 1981.

Another bit of irony on this issue is what happened to advertising expenditures. According to Schneider, Klein, and Murphy, these expenditures reached a peak in 1967, then declined slightly and fell sharply in 1971 and 1972. Thus, the initial impact of the ban was to make the fight for brand share less costly. By 1976, however, advertising in other areas than television and radio increased to the point where expenditures exceeded their 1967 peak.

Impacts of a Change in Demand

Apparently, consumer response to the health issue is resulting in a leftward shift of the demand curve for tobacco. Present and contemplated governmental policy is abetting this process. If government pricing policy keeps shrinking the U.S. market share of tobacco sales abroad, demand there will also fall. Therefore it is likely that the total demand for cigarette tobacco will fall over time. A question that arises in such a situation is what happens not only to producers, but to other industries complementary to tobacco and cigarette production. Some analyses point to a fall in tax receipts, reduced employment in farm machinery production and sales, and so on. In the judgment of the author, most of these analyses are overdrawn. Since tobacco production and manufacturing are so specialized, it is fairly easy to determine resource use, and to draw some inferences about changes.

The author first looked at this problem in 1972 (Johnson, 1972). Some of what follows is an update of that material. We can distinguish between the case of a rapid fall to zero consumption and that of a gradual decline in demand brought about by a governmental ban, for example. The former is less likely than the latter, so only the gradual decline is really considered. The only real difference would be in the speed of adjustment.

Relative declines in particular industries are not all that uncommon. Any good with an income elasticity of less than 1.0 will decline relative to all goods as real income rises. Thus domestic food consumption and all agricultural products will see a relative decline over time. Absolute declines may not be as prevalent, although other agricultural products such as flax, oats, and cotton have undergone such declines. The economy survived these incidents. Some caused more pain than others, but the adjustments took place.

There are few lamentations for mule traders or harness workers heard these days. That is not so because they were insignificant to the economy at the time that automobiles and tractors arrived; it is true because the long run has come and gone for them. Predictions about tobacco are difficult because economists do not measure length of run in terms of ordinary units of time. They measure it in terms of how long it takes for all factors in a particular use to become variable rather than fixed. Roughly speaking, that condition would be achieved when rents ceased to accrue to such factors as the ability to judge mules, for example, and the pens and corrals of traders either were depreciated in value to zero or reverted to an alternative use. At this point, potential factors in mule trading will only earn their opportunity cost and can be put to their next most productive use.

The same process will operate in industries where the demand does not fall as close to zero as in mule breeding and handling. Rents to specific factors fall so that resources move out, or at least new ones do not enter, and factor prices fall to their opportunity costs. The concept of rent being used here holds that in the short run supply functions of some factors will be upward sloping, and the average payment to the factor will be greater than the alternative opportunity cost of all but the marginal unit. These payments in excess of opportunity costs are rents to the factor involved.

The problem is that the intensity and duration of the adjustment process is clearly going to depend on the kind of industry, the kinds of factors employed, and governmental policy involved. What features of the tobacco industry that affect this process?

Several problems arise in connection with multiplier effects of structural changes. One has to do with length of run. As pointed out earlier, in the long run all resources can be reallocated. Labor can be retrained, persons with job-specific skills will retire, and there will be no employment effects of the change. There should be relatively little disagreement on this point. The more important question has to do with the size of any short-run multiplier effect.

The economy is a general equilibrium system; all markets are interconnected. When the economy as a whole is broken down into smaller units such as states and cities, these interconnections become even clearer. Take, for example, a small town with one manufacturing plant as the major employer. If the factory should shut down, then it seems obvious that many employees in addition to those directly affected, would be hurt also. The bank, the stores, and other services would be affected. The same notion is used in reverse by local and state "industry hunters" to predict employment effects of attracting new industries. The basic question, which is empirical, not theoretical, concerns the size of any such short-run employment multipliers.

A somewhat dated but highly relevant example may help to shed some light on this empirical question (see Johnson 1972). In mid 1968 in the Seattle-Everett, Washington, area total employment was 553,000 persons. Of these, 171,000 were employed in manufacturing. A large fraction of these manufacturing employees worked for the Boeing Aircraft Company. In 1969 a decision was made not to build the SST aircraft, for which Boeing was the prime contractor.

By February 1971, the number of manufacturing employees had fallen to 109,000—a drop of 36 percent. Total employment in February 1971 was 487,000—a decline of 12 percent. That is, manufacturing employment fell by 62,000 jobs, while total employment fell by 66,000. The unemployment rate rose from 4.3 to 12 percent. This occurred at the same time that national unemployment was rising from 4.3 percent to close to 6 percent, thus jobs were also scarcer than they had been previously in other areas where mobile workers might go. The shock in Seattle, large by any standard, did not multiply itself in terms of jobs lost in other fields in three years.

Nothing in the preceding illustration is meant to imply that the citizens of Seattle were as well off as before; 66,000 jobs had been lost. Even if the job loss did not multiply, incomes of others might be lower than just the salaries of the laid-off workers. The point is that if one does not observe multiplier effects from the SST cancellation, one will be hard pressed to find them elsewhere in middle-sized to large metropolitan areas. Cigarette manufacturing facilities are in cities like Louisville, Kentucky, Richmond, Virginia, and Winston-Salem, North Carolina. Even in the last city mentioned, R. J. Reynolds does not employ as large a fraction of the work force as Boeing did in Seattle. Shrinking the work force in cigarette manufacturing is not apt to shrink the work force in general by more than the immediate loss.

With reasonably full employment and a reasonably well functioning price system, a shift in demand away from a product means that income is being spent elsewhere, and factors will tend to be reallocated from that one product to others. In this case, no capital or jobs are lost overall. There will be costs and returns from this rearrangement, so let us look at some of these short-run adjustments.

Consider first the manufacturing of tobacco products. Presumably the main focus should be on cigarettes because the demand functions for cigars and pipe tobacco are expected to be more stable, and less subject to interference than that for cigarettes. One would expect that sudden losses to shareholders in the major cigarette companies would not elicit too many tears from the public at large, but there would be other losses caused by a leftward shift in demand.

Cigarette manufacturing is a relatively capital-intensive industry. This capital intensity means that highly specialized machines are the most fixed asset of the firms involved. Some labor associated with this machinery is also earning rent from being employed here rather than elsewhere. The average hourly wage in cigarette manufacturing is just about equal to the U.S. average hourly wage, and is above that of the average production worker in nondurable manufacturing. The inference from this would be that there are some rents being earned, but the number of workers earning them is not known. Most of the white collar workers—secretaries, clerks, bookkeepers, and so on—would probably be earning no rents at all.

The total number of jobs involved is not large. The number of workers who would suffer large sudden losses is not large either. The fixed factors in manufacturing, then, would appear to be machinery and a small amount of labor. While some analysts predict a multiplier effect from a job loss of this nature, this study takes the opposite point of view.

The next stage is the marketing and distribution of raw tobacco. In this stage are auctioning, warehousing, and stemming and redrying. The redrying is not as capital intensive as manufacturing, but there will be some fixed items of capital that would suffer sudden losses. Average wage rates reported for stemming and redrying are barely above the minimum wage. Few employees at this wage level can be considered fixed to the industry.

The warehousing activity is one that appears to have been earning rents. Institutional arrangements have been such that a casual observer concludes that entry is limited. The asset that is fixed and earning rents, whether it be the warehouse itself or some other attribute of the process, belongs to the warehouse owners. Again, the number of such owners is not large, and the dollar value of potential losses is simply not available. In addition to warehouse owners, there are some skilled auctioneers and buyers who are potential losers. This is also a very small group of people.

We turn now to the stage in the process where potential losers are most readily identified. At the level of farm production, the fixed factor is obviously land (and certain equipment), and, under current programs more specifically, allotments. Very little, if any, labor can be considered fixed to tobacco in the sense of rents accruing to occupational skills.

In summary, then, we have identified certain factors that will bear the brunt of short-run adjustments to a decline in demand for tobacco. These factors are those that are presumed to be earning rents or to represent assets that are capitalized rents. A decline in demand will impose sudden losses on holders of such assets as specialized machinery and labor in cigarette manufacturing, warehouses, and tobacco production allotments. The process is one whereby adjustments take place in response to changes in demand. These adjustments are equilibrating, with respect to allocative efficiency, and the end result is to change the income distribution.

Much of the adjustment postulated above has already taken place. All of the major cigarette companies are now diversified conglomerates. None of them are wholly dependent on cigarette sales, as they were 20 years ago.

In the farm production of tobacco, the asset generating rents is the quota or allotment—the right to grow tobacco. The value of a quota depends in part on where it is located, since tobacco allotment cannot be leased across county lines. Before lease and transfer came into effect, the only way to acquire the right to grow was to buy the farm on which tobacco was grown. The value of the quota could be fairly accurately determined by comparing the sale price of tobacco farms with nontobacco farms with the same characteristics. With lease and transfer, observed rental rates could be capitalized to indicate value. This was only true for a few years, however. The rental contracts are annual ones, and the short-run right to grow tobacco can diverge from the perceived value of the quota. The comparison of tobacco and nontobacco farms can still be utilized.

A careful study by Seagraves and Williams (1981) made such a comparison. They had access to data from actual sales from 1975 to 1980. Their estimating technique placed the value of a pound of allotment at $3.50 in 1975, rising to $4.61 in 1977, and falling to $3.24 in 1980. In constant dollars, adjusting for inflation, they conclude that the value fell by 40 percent from 1975 to 1980. Apparently the average expectation about the life of the program was declining. If the support price had stayed in place as a guarantee, one would expect the allotments' values to hold up.

This discrepancy between the value of the current right to produce and the value of the permanent right to produce can be seen another way. Since the permanent right to produce can now be bought or sold, one ought to be able to infer from the sale price either the flow rent—if the discount rate is known—or the discount rate, if the rent is known. Presumably, the discount rate will include expectations about the life of the price program.

Not much data are available for sale prices of quotas. The quoted price in newspapers have typically been under $3.00 per pound. Rents have been running up to 60 cents per pound. This means the discount rate is over 20 percent—well above the long-term interest rates. Either current, short-run rents are out of equilibrium with long-run rents, or the expected life of the program on average is quite short.

One would expect the value of allotments to fall even more as a result of the 1982 legislation. The new law allows the secretary of agriculture to raise the support price by less than the amount called for by the formula. Specifically, he can make the increase as small as 65 percent of the formula increase. The new law also places an assessment on the marketing of tobacco. This assessment is to cover the operating costs of the stabilization cooperatives, as they no longer have access to nonrecourse loans from the Commodity Credit Corporation. (They can still borrow at the market rate from the CCC.) Then not only will the support price put a lower floor under the market price, the realized market price will be lower when the assessment is factored out. The value of production rights can only move lower.

5

STRUCTURAL CHANGES IN FARMING

Introduction

All farming operations have seen a revolutionary change in technology in the 50 years since the tobacco program first went into effect. In tobacco, however, many changes were slow in coming. This slowness was due to the supply control program, with its inherent restrictions on the size of operations. When the changes did come, they put severe pressure on the program—especially that for flue-cured.

Historically tobacco has been a highly labor-intensive crop. Tobacco is sold by leaves, so at some point the leaf must be separated from the stalk. The time at which this is done varies by the type of tobacco, but in any event it has to be done. Other labor-using tasks have been getting tobacco into the barn for the curing process, preparing it for market, and the transplanting operation in the spring. In addition, of course, there are the operations associated with any crop, such as land preparation, cultivation, and physical delivery to the market. As a consequence of this labor intensity, tobacco tended to be grown on small units. In the burley regions, these were typically farms much smaller than those in the corn belt, for example. Where tobacco farming was combined with other commercial enterprises, the size of the tobacco operation was limited by the amount of family labor available. In the flue-cured areas tobacco was grown in relatively small units, as in burley, or as a small unit of a larger multiple-unit enterprise. This latter utilized the sharecropping system, which was also commonly found in cotton culture in the South. The sharecropper was responsible for a small unit of a larger farm. A standard arrangement might be that for a fraction of the crop, from one fourth to one half, the owner would furnish the land and a share of the operating expenses. In addition to the land, the sharecropper got a house, a garden plot, and perhaps some pasture and pen space for hogs. Usually the sharecropper was also receiving some interest payment, since he was probably extended credit for expenses with below-market interest payments on the loan.

A large literature on southern sharecropping exists. Tobacco presents no special problems for the institution. At the time when the tobacco program was put in place, the institution of sharecropping was a stable process for producing certain crops. It was not until well after World War II that changes in sharecropping occurred. One item of interest for both tobacco and cotton was that the allotment of acres for control of production went with the land. Therefore the owner of the land "owned" the production rights granted by the program. The share tenant, then, shared in the higher prices, but also in any acreage reduction, but did not share in any price increase in the land that resulted from the production restriction. In a typical flue-cured multiple unit operation, the owner usually produced some tobacco on his own and also leased out production on shares. This type of operation is by no means gone completely, but changes in the production process have affected the pattern of labor use.

Changes in the Demand for Labor

The changes in labor requirements have been most dramatic in flue-cured tobacco. Tables 5.1–5.4 are reproduced from enterprise budgets prepared by tobacco specialists at North Carolina State University. Table 5.1 is a budget showing per-acre labor requirements in 1952. Table 5.2 shows per-acre labor requirements in 1983 for a large farm (40 or more acres of tobacco). Table 5.3 shows the same information for a small farm (10 acres or less of tobacco). Table 5.4 is the 1983 estimated labor per acre of burley tobacco in North Carolina. The most dramatic comparison, of course, is that between the 1952 budget and the 1983 large farm budget. Even the comparison of the 1952 budget to 1983 small farm budget shows fairly sharp changes. These comparisons show the results of a 30-year transition from one technology to another. The 1983 numbers are the result of an evolutionary process. None of the changes were so sudden that a new system was adopted in as little time as a year, for example. We will now examine the budgets, note the changes, and try to fill in the history as we proceed.

Although one might think that the use of animal power had ceased by 1950, Table 5.1 notes the requirement of a mule. This seems especially striking since this budget is for flue-cured tobacco in general, and not just for small or poor farms. This use of mules is, in fact, not unrelated to the tobacco program. It was then an acreage reduction program, so the grower's objective was to increase yields as much as possible. Plant and row spacing had a critical impact on yield, and mules were less apt to bruise tobacco leaves than was a tractor. Therefore, mules continued in use until the administration of the program permitted some adjustments in acreage that changed row spacing, and made the use of tractors for cultivating and harvesting viable. Mules were replaced before the greater technological advances of the 1970s. As long as harvesting was done by hand, the substitution of tractors for mules did not reduce harvest labor all that much.

The first operation shown in Tables 5.1–5.4 is that of the plant bed. Tobacco is seeded in a plant bed, and then plants are transplanted from the bed to the field where they are grown. This two-stage planting operation is labor intensive even under modern conditions. The number of hours of labor required has been reduced from 22 to 3.4 between 1952 and 1983 (Tables 5.1 and 5.2). The proportion of total labor hours, however, has not changed that much—from 4.6 percent in 1952 to 3.4 percent in 1983. With modern equipment, land preparation requires fewer hours, but even in 1952, land preparation was not a particularly heavy user of labor, using only 2.5 percent of total labor.

Transplanting continues to be a labor-intensive operation. The 1983 budget shows the use of a transplanter machine, but it is still necessary to place the plants in the ground by hand. Pulling the plants from the plant bed is strictly a hand operation. This labor intensity is demonstrated by the fact that while hours required in 1983 were only one half that of 1952, they represented 16.4 percent of total hours, up from 7.15 percent in 1952. The growing operation has also changed. The fields are cultivated fewer times, for instance. The major change, however, has been the development and adoption of a chemical process for sucker control. In the growing process the tobacco plant is topped, that is, the flower bud is removed, in order to force growth into the leaves, rather than have the plant grow higher. Topping causes secondary growth, suckers, to appear where leaves join the stalk. These suckers must be removed so they will not rob the leaves of nutrients. Technological developments reduced this topping and suckering labor use from 24 to 1.25 hours.

One of the greatest changes in labor requirements has occurred in the harvest operation. The budgets show that harvest and marketing labor has fallen from 365 hours in 1952 to 74 hours for a large farm, and 156 for a small farm in 1983. Note first that not all this change is related to new equipment. The third item in the 1952 budget under harvesting lists grading and tying at 140 hours per acre. That is only slightly lower than the 165 hours required to remove physically the leaves from the field. Prior to 1968 in flue-cured markets, other than Georgia-Florida, tobacco was tied into hands of about 20 to 30 leaves before it was brought to market. This tying took place simultaneously with the sorting into grades. The various grades were then placed into burlap sheets and taken to market. In 1968 all flue-cured belts were allowed to market tobacco loose-leaf. At least in part this change was endogenous. In traditional curing the tobacco was hung on sticks, while in the new bulk-barn curing opera-

TABLE 5.1
Average Labor Requirements per Acre for Flue-Cured Tobacco with Partial Mechanization, 1952

	Labor and Power (hours per acre)		
Operation	Man	Mule	Tractor
Plant bed (preparation, planting, and care)	22.0	2.5	.5
Preplanting			
Cover crop	1.4		1.0
Cutting stalks	1.1	2.2	
Breaking	1.3		1.3
Disking	.9		.9
Harrowing	.5		.5
Laying off rows	.6		.6
Distributing fertilizer	2.8	1.9	
Ridging rows	3.0	3.0	
Total	11.6	7.1	4.8
Transplanting	35.0	5.0	
Growing after planting			
Hoeing	8.5		
Cultivating	12.0	12.0	
Applying side-dressing	1.5		
Applying poison	2.0	1.5	
Topping, suckering, and worming	24.0		
Total	48.0	13.5	
Harvesting and preparing for market			
Harvesting	165.0	30.0	
Curing (taking out, ordering, and so on)	50.0		
Grading and tying	140.0		
Total	355.0	30.0	
Marketing	10.0		
Total all labor	481.6	53.1	4.8

Source: Pierce and Williams 1952.

TABLE 5.2
Tobacco, Flue-Cured: 1983 Estimated Total Labor and Power Inputs per Acre; Large Farm (40 acres or more)

Month	Type of Operation	Equipment Used	Hours/Acre	
			Labor	Power
	Plant bed (70 sq. yd.)			
January	Plowing	4-bottom plow	0.05	0.03
	Disking	20' disk	0.01	0.01
	Fumigating	Custom hired	—	—
February	Fertilizing, raking, seeding	Pickup truck	2.15	0.10
March	Top-dressing	Pickup truck	1.97	0.25
	Pest control	Sprayer	0.20	0.18
	Land preparation			
	Plowing	4-bottom plow	0.52	0.47
April	Disking	20' disk	0.12	0.11
	Harrowing	18' section harrow	0.17	0.16
	Applying chemicals	Sprayer	0.20	0.18
	Transplanting			
	Pulling plants	Hand	7.00	—
May	Hauling plants	Pickup truck	1.20	1.00
	Hauling water	2-ton truck with water tank	1.20	1.00
	Transplanting and fertilizing	4-row transplanter	7.00	0.87
	Growing			
	Cultivating, 2 times	4-row rolling cultivator	0.33	0.30

78

Month	Operation	Equipment		
June	Cultivating, side dressing	4-row rolling cultivator	0.16	0.14
	Applying pesticides, 3 times	Sprayer	1.20	1.10
June–July	Topping, sucker control, 3 times	Tractor mounted topper and sprayer	1.25	1.13
July–August	Harvesting, curing, marketing			
	Mechanical harvesting, 6 times	1-row harvester	7.83	6.45
	Hauling to barn	Pickup truck and trailer	7.20	6.00
	Bulk-racking	Bulk barns	26.00	—
	Loading barn		15.00	—
	Curing supervision	Pickup truck	2.40	2.00
	Sheeting	2-ton truck to packhouse	10.40	2.00
July–September	Marketing	2-ton truck	5.20	2.80
September	Postharvest:			
	Plowing	6-bottom plow	0.52	0.47
	Stalk destruction, 2 times	20' disk	0.23	0.21
	Seeding cover crop	Grain drill	0.26	0.24
Total			99.77	

Source: Pugh and Collins 1983.

TABLE 5.3
Tobacco, Flue-Cured: 1983 Estimated Total Labor and Power Inputs per Acre; Small Farm (10 acres or less)

Month	Type of Operation	Equipment Used	Hours/Acre Labor	Hours/Acre Power
January	Plant bed (100 sq. yd.)			
	Plowing	3-bottom plow	0.09	0.08
	Disking	8' disk	0.03	0.03
	Fumigating	Custom hired	—	—
February	Fertilizing, raking, seeding	Pickup truck	2.40	2.00
March	Pest control, 6 times	Sprayer	0.12	0.11
	Top-dressing	Pickup truck	1.20	1.00
	Land preparation (1¼ acres per acre of allotment)			
	Plowing	3-bottom plow	1.11	1.01
	Disking, 2 times	8' disk	0.82	0.74
April	Harrowing	Section harrow, 13'	0.22	0.20
	Applying nematicide	Sprayer or applicator	0.25	0.22
	Disking	8' disk	0.41	0.37
	Applying herbicide	Sprayer or applicator	0.25	0.22
	Laying-off rows and fertilizing	1-row disk-hiller	0.89	0.81
May	Transplanting			
	Pulling plants	Hand	8.00	—
	Hauling plants and water	Pickup truck	1.20	1.00

80

	Operation	Equipment		
	Transplanting	1-row transplanter	12.38	3.49
	Growing			
June	Cultivating, 2 times	1-row rolling cultivator	1.30	1.18
	Cultivating, side-dressing	1-row rolling cultivator with fertilizer attachment, pickup truck	0.65	0.59
			1.20	1.00
	Laying-by herbicide	4-row sprayer	0.20	0.18
June–July	Apply insecticides, 2 times	4-row sprayer	0.40	0.36
	Topping	Hand	10.00	—
	Applying sucker control, 2 times	4-row sprayer	0.40	0.36
	Harvesting, curing, marketing			
July–August	Priming	Hand	52.00	—
	Hauling to barn	Trailer and pickup truck	14.00	4.00
	Barn preparation	Tying machine	38.00	—
	Loading barn	Conventional barns	19.00	—
	Curing supervision		2.00	—
	Removal and sheeting	Pickup truck	23.00	2.00
July–September	Marketing	Pickup truck	7.80	4.00
	Postharvest			
September	Cutting stalks	1-row cutter	0.31	0.28
	Plowing	3-bottom plow	1.11	1.01
	Disking, 2 times	8' disk	0.82	0.74
	Seeding cover crop	Grain drill	0.50	0.45
Total			202.06	

Source: Pugh and Collins 1983.

TABLE 5.4
Tobacco, Burley: 1983 Estimated Total Labor and Power Inputs per Acre

Month	Type of Operation	Equipment Used	Hours/Acre	
			Total Labor	Power Only
October	Plowing plant bed	1-bottom plow	0.35	0.31
	Disking plant bed	8' disk	0.09	0.06
	Harrowing plant bed	Section harrow	0.04	0.02
	Preparing bed for fumigating	Methyl bromide applicator	7.80	—
March	Raking, fertilizing and seeding plant bed	Hand	3.00	—
	Watering	Hand and hand sprayer	2.50	—
April	Plant bed care		2.00	—
	Plowing field	1-bottom plow	3.47	3.15
	Disking field, 2 times	8' disk	0.65	0.59
May	Plant bed care	Hand	2.00	—
	Broadcasting fertilizer and nitrogen	Spreader	0.31	0.28
	Disking in fertilizer	8' disk	0.33	0.30
	Harrowing	Section harrow	0.17	0.16
	Pulling plants	Hand	10.00	—
	Hauling plants and water	Pickup truck	2.04	1.70
	Transplanting into field	1-row transplanter	12.16	3.49
May–June	Applying herbicide	4-row sprayer	0.40	0.36

Month	Operation	Method/Equipment		
June	Hoeing	Hand	4.00	—
June–July	Applying pesticide, (1 time)	Hand sprayer	4.00	—
	Cultivating, 3 times	1-row cultivator	3.90	3.54
	Applying contact	Hand sprayer	6.00	—
August	Topping and suckering	Hand	8.00	—
	Applying systemic chemical	Hand sprayer	6.00	—
September	Cutting and placing on sticks	Hand	40.00	—
	Hauling and hanging in barn	Pickup truck	40.00	10.00
September–October	Attending curing process		4.00	—
October	Disking out roots for cover crop, 2 times	8' disk	0.58	0.53
	Seeding cover crop	Grain drill	0.40	0.36
October–December	Stripping, grading and baling	Hand, baler	60.00	—
November–December	Marketing	Pickup truck	9.00	7.50
Total			233.19	

Source: Pugh and Collins 1983.

tion, the leaves are placed in racks. It is much simpler to sheet the tobacco loose-leaf directly from the barn. The labor reduction in this change was quite large. Thus, a large part of the change in labor requirements came from a simple administrative change in the market process. Contrary to popular impression, the technological change in harvesting and curing was not solely responsible for the change in labor requirements.

As can be seen from the budgets, harvest labor fell from 165 hours per acre in 1952 to 55 hours on large farms in 1983. This change is so dramatic that the process should be described in some detail, for those not familiar with tobacco culture. Two basic requirements had to be met before tobacco harvest could be mechanized. First, the acreage necessary to take advantage of machinery had to be acquired. Before lease and transfer made such an acquisition possible, it was simply not feasible for a sufficient number of farmers to have the acreage to make machinery pay. Second, machinery had to be developed that would not injure the crop. Tobacco is very sensitive to bruising, and field loss could offset potential gains. With the coming of lease and transfer the size problem was solved, and the injury problem became simply a technical problem of machinery development.

In the traditional harvest method, workers picked individual leaves from the plant, a process variously called cropping, priming, or other names. These leaves were placed on a sled that a mule dragged between the rows. In July and August this was a hot, laborious, and time consuming operation. After the priming operation the leaves were tied on sticks and hung in a relatively small barn, often 16 feet square. The tobacco was then cured by heat drawn by flues from an exterior heat source through the barn. This temperature varied with the time the tobacco had been in the barn, and required close attention. The tobacco was taken from the barn when cured, and the tying and grading process started. This whole priming operation was then repeated as the leaves matured in succession along the stalk.

The modern mechanical harvester is a self-propelled machine that removes the leaves from the plant at the appropriate height. The leaves are dropped to a conveyòr belt, which takes them to a hopper. When the hopper is full, it is taken to the barning area. There the leaves are placed in a rack, which, when full, is closed by metal props on the lid being forced through the tobacco. This barn is a metal structure that has roughly the same capacity as the traditional curing barn; one barn handles three acres. The curing system is much different, however. The leaves are placed on racks, but in random order. The racks go into the barn in a denser fashion than that used in conventional curing barns. The curing heat is forced through the tobacco by a fan. Loading and unloading the barn is still physical work requiring stamina, but fewer hours are required and less supervision of the curing process itself is required. Note that the budget for medium farms also includes bulk barns, but does not include a mechanical harvester. Whatever efficiencies are associated with the bulk curing process alone are available without the harvester. A minimum of about 40 acres is still required to make the harvester pay off.

Now, look at the burley budget. Burley production requires more labor than flue-cured, even if one considers the small flue-cured operation. There are many differences between burley and flue-cured tobacco production. Some of these account for the lesser degree of mechanization found in burley, as opposed to flue-cured. The average burley allotment, for one thing, is much smaller than the average flue-cured allotment. Many burley allotments are less than an acre in size, and such small units do not lend themselves to mechanization. Second, the harvesting of burley does not lend itself to mechanization: The whole plant is cut, and the field operation is only done once. The plants are then placed on sticks, taken to a large, dry but airy barn where the whole plant is hung to cure. In about six weeks to two months the plant is taken down, and the leaves stripped off one by one. They are then graded, as is done with flue-cured. The one significant difference in burley is that, although the tying requirement is now gone—as it is in flue-cured—the burley leaves are compressed into a rectangular bale, and marketed this way, rather than loose-leaf. This is labor saving, but it has not caused as dramatic a change as loose-leaf marketing did with flue-cured tobacco.

An Income Distribution Problem

The mechanization of flue-cured tobacco harvesting and the lease and transfer program described earlier are intimately related. The lease and transfer program allowed growers of tobacco to acquire units large enough to take advantage of mechanical harvesting equipment. Some operators in the flat coastal plains area are leasing—on an annual basis—many more pounds of quota than they own. Since quota can be leased only within a county, the amount available for lease is limited. As a consequence of this scarcity, operators in some counties bid up the rental rate for quota to a level where the lessee probably does not receive any return on the quota. Since the lessees are presumably the superior managers, they are still earning rents for their managerial skills and their human and physical capital. The situation has led to a conflict between lessors and lessees over the distribution of income from tobacco production.

Prior to lease and transfer and mechanization, there was usually no conflict among growers of tobacco. This new situation meant that the owner of the quota and the renter of that quota now were on different sides of a market. The lease transaction is a market transaction. Individuals simply bargain among themselves and make private controls at agreed-upon prices. The owners of quota may be, for example, retired persons, heirs of previous owners, or persons more interested in a nonfarm occupation. The typical renter of large amounts of quota will be a skilled grower with a large investment in equipment. During the 1970s, some antagonism between these groups arose. The feeling on the part of the growers was that rents were increasing, and they were having to pay "unproductive" owners more than they ought. There are two fallacies with respect to this position. One, already mentioned, is that the rental agreement is a market phenomenon governed by the forces of supply and demand. The second is that the real rental rate had not been increasing. As noted in Chapter 3, the real price of tobacco has stayed remarkably constant in real terms. Rents had been increasing in nominal terms also, but had not increased in constant dollars. Pugh and Hoover (1981) show this by taking rent as a percentage of price over time. This percentage did not change over the decade of the 1970s.

The antagonism continued nonetheless. In considering new tobacco legislation in 1982, a difference of opinion among tobacco interests could be heard for the first time. One provision of that legislation was probably the result of renters' concerns. The law required institutional holders of quota to sell it. Individuals were free to sell, but banks, power companies, and so on, had to sell. The matter is by no means resolved as of this writing. If the program continues in its current form, the conflict will continue. This is not as much of a problem in burley areas, since there is much less mechanization and much less lease and transfer activity with that crop.

Economic Consequences of Changing Labor Requirements

As noted above, some of the labor demand changes in tobacco production are endogenous and represent responses to program changes; some are endogenous and represent responses to market phenomena (for example, real wage increases); some simply represent use of improved machinery in the tobacco enterprise. These endogenous changes, in general, have come gradually. The flow of labor from tobacco production to other pursuits does not appear to put undue strain on labor markets. Another possibility exists, however. Suppose there is a technological breakthrough, and a mechanized process changes relative costs so much that labor is displaced rapidly and local and regional labor markets cannot easily absorb displaced workers. This classic identification problem has been much discussed in terms of whether farm workers are drawn off the farm, or whether they are pushed out. Some elements of both effects are, of course, present.

The number of farmers in the United States peaked in 1920. Since then, with the exception of some years during the Great Depression of the 1930s, the exodus from farms to urban areas has continued unabated. The movement was quite dramatic during the 1950s. One of the big flows out of agriculture was the flight of laborers from cotton farms to urban areas, especially to northern urban areas. Many observers saw this flow of sharecroppers and laborers as the result of workers being pushed off farms as a result of the adoption of the mechanized cotton picker. They viewed this as a social problem of some magnitude. Workers were displaced, moved to the city, and created a burden for municipal, state, and other physical and social service providers. There is no doubt about the flow itself, although it could only be documented through census observations of the number of farms and farmers in cotton growing regions. The actual impact on cities is more difficult to assess. Regardless of the magnitude of the problem, the possibility of a repetition of the process came to be feared by the late 1960s. Workable tobacco harvesters had been developed, and the means to consolidate production units had been put in place. The concern was that the flue-cured tobacco region would see the same kind of displacement of labor that was alleged to have occurred in cotton. Many people saw this as the last great push of poor blacks off the soil.

In 1971 the New York Times ran a front page story on the likelihood of black workers being displaced. In the winter of 1972 the U.S. Department of Labor held a two day regional meeting in Raleigh, North Carolina, to discuss the issues. What impact would a large flow of labor from tobacco production have on the workers themselves, on the labor force in the region, and on social institutions? The impact of such a flow would depend critically on the magnitude of the flow and the length of time the process took. In connection with the latter problem there was reason to be sanguine. Many studies of adoption of new technologies had shown that most of them, both in agriculture and industry, had taken considerable time from the placement of the first machines until some proportion approaching 90 percent of potential users had adopted them. This pattern had been true of the cotton picker; while the number who had left was large, they did not all leave in one year—or even ten. There was no reason to believe that the adoption pattern in tobacco would be any different. Subsequent events have shown this to be the case. By 1982, ten years from the Labor Department meeting, less than half of the flue-cured crop was being harvested by mechanical harvesters.

Ironically, the other problem, the size of the flow had already been observed in part. As we saw earlier loose-leaf sales were first permitted in 1968. That meant that any farm could save 130 hours per acre from that marketing change alone—somewhere between a third and a half of the hours eventually to be lost, and this had already taken place without much notice in the press. In any event, the Department of Labor commissioned a study to assess the magnitude of the problem, to be undertaken in conjunction by the U.S.

Department of Agriculture and North Carolina State University. The major effort in that study was a sample survey of workers and households of workers in the tobacco growing region of eastern North Carolina, where tobacco is most important. Results of such a study should be applicable to similar areas in South Carolina and Georgia. From information about workers, their characteristics, their employment on and off the farm, and labor market conditions in the area, one should be able to predict the impact from the release of labor from tobacco harvesting. The results of the study were published in an Economics Research Report from the Department of Economics and Business, North Carolina State University in June 1977 (Hoover and Perkinson 1977).

Some of the characteristics of the persons sampled in 1972 are shown in Tables 5.5–5.7. As we have seen, the major use of labor is harvest labor. This is a seasonal demand of about two months' duration. Thus, there is a large number of hired workers. The interesting aspect of the hired workers is their youth; more than half are under 18. Since the duration of employment is quite short, total earnings of harvest workers are not all that much. An adoption of mechanization that released harvest workers would release teenagers, and not family breadwinners. If we look at harvest workers on their own farm, the racial breakdown in the study area was fairly evenly divided between blacks and whites. A release of small farmers from this group would affect family earnings, but the impact would not be large. The study predicted that the loss would be 7 percent of income from the average household with complete adoption by 1980. So the major conclusion was that by 1980 the total impact of complete mechanization of the harvest process would not be large.

We have now passed the 1980 projection date of the study, and we can assess in very rough fashion what happened. The prediction was that tobacco mechanization would not alter the farm migration pattern very much, and impact on the area's labor supply and demand would not be very great either. As well as can be detected, these predictions have been borne out. There have been no more journalistic accounts of the impact on migration flows or unemployment. Eastern North Carolina seems no more affected by unemployment or social ills than other areas. Nonfarm employment has in-

TABLE 5.5
Characteristics of Hired Tobacco Harvest Workers by Race and Sex, 1972

Item	Unit	Black		White		Total
		Female	Male	Female	Male	
Number of workers	No.	7,837	5,537	2,911	3,047	19,332
Distribution	Pct.	40.5	28.6	15.1	15.7	100.0
Harvest hours	1,000	2,046	1,627	633	652	4,058
Distribution	Pct.	41.3	32.8	12.8	13.2	100.0
Harvest earnings	$1,000	2,522	2,398	778	906	6,604
Distribution	Pct.	38.2	36.3	11.8	13.7	100.0
Total earnings	$1,000	4,942	5,355	1,161	1,816	13,274
Distribution	Pct.	37.2	40.3	8.7	13.7	100.0
Average harvest hours	Hrs.	261	294	217	214	256
Average harvest earnings	Dol.	322	433	267	297	342
Average hourly wage	Dol.	1.32	1.47	1.23	1.39	1.33
Average total earnings	Dol.	631	967	399	596	687
Harvest earnings share	Pct.	51.0	44.8	67.0	49.9	49.8
Average age	Yrs.	32.4	21.4	24.3	19.5	26.0
Less than 18	Pct.	33.5	59.1	54.3	78.3	51.0
Average education	Yrs.	8.5	8.9	9.8	8.5	8.8
Primary adult	Pct.	51.6	13.5	36.1	9.0	31.6
Married	Pct.	33.8	12.2	29.5	8.9	23.0

Source: Hoover and Perkinson 1977.

TABLE 5.6
Characteristics of Own-Farm Tobacco Harvest Workers by Race and Sex, 1972

Item	Unit	Black		White		Total
		Female	Male	Female	Male	
Number	No.	2,476	3,384	2,868	4,232	12,960
Distribution	Pct.	19.1	26.1	22.1	32.6	100.0
Harvest Hours	1,000	625	1,441	1,152	2,722	5,940
Distribution	Pct.	10.5	24.3	19.4	45.8	100.0
Harvest earnings	$1,000	794	2,116	1,419	3,887	8,216
Distribution	Pct.	9.7	25.8	17.3	47.3	100.0
Total earnings	$1,000	2,280	7,636	4,424	16,330	30,670
Distribution	Pct.	7.4	24.9	14.4	53.2	100.0
Average harvest hours	Hrs.	253	426	402	643	458
Average harvest earnings	Dol.	321	625	495	919	634
Average hourly wage	Dol.	1.27	1.47	1.23	1.43	1.38
Average total earnings	Dol.	921	2,256	1,543	3,859	2,367
Harvest earnings share	Pct.	34.8	27.7	32.1	23.8	26.8
Average age	Yrs.	33.8	37.5	34.4	41.2	37.3
Less than 18	Pct.	32.2	30.2	25.4	9.7	22.8
Average education	Yrs.	8.8	7.5	9.8	9.5	8.9
Primary adult	Pct.	52.4	55.4	64.0	75.9	63.4
Married	Pct.	47.5	51.4	65.3	69.8	59.7

Source: Hoover and Perkinson 1977.

TABLE 5.7
Percentage Distribution of Own-Farm Harvest Workers by the
Relative Importance of Harvest Earnings in 1972 and Other
Worker Characteristics

	Harvest Earnings Share of Total Earnings				
Worker Characteristics	*Less than 25%*	*25–49%*	*50–74%*	*75% or more*	*Total*
Age					
12–13	9.4	20.3	9.7	60.7	100.0
14–15	12.6	24.2	—	63.3	100.0
16–17	12.1	20.8	21.4	45.7	100.0
18–24	22.9	26.7	13.6	36.8	100.0
25–44	41.1	34.1	12.8	12.0	100.0
45–55	48.5	33.0	9.0	9.5	100.0
55–64	49.5	28.2	7.0	15.2	100.0
65 +	55.2	20.2	14.4	10.1	100.0
Level of earnings					
Less than $100	74.7	2.3	2.0	21.0	100.0
$100–249	33.4	22.2	5.8	38.6	100.0
$250–499	31.8	29.1	10.2	28.8	100.0
$500–749	40.8	23.2	18.1	17.9	100.0
$750–999	29.1	44.2	19.6	7.0	100.0
$1,000–1,249	27.5	56.8	10.0	5.7	100.0
$1,250 +	4.7	48.7	15.0	31.6	100.0
Race/Sex					
Black female	28.1	21.2	10.6	40.0	100.0
Black male	30.9	44.1	7.6	17.5	100.0
White female	29.4	13.9	15.8	40.8	100.0
White male	48.6	30.3	11.1	10.0	100.0
All workers	35.8	28.5	11.1	24.5	100.0

Source: Hoover and Perkinson 1977.

creased in the area. The transition, as was predicted, has been
gradual. Market forces seem to have facilitated the adjustment quite
well.

In fact, a somewhat startling change has occurred in labor utilization in eastern North Carolina and South Carolina. The eastern seaboard of the United States has long had migratory labor moving up from Florida to New York as the season progressed. These workers have typically been associated with labor-intensive operations such as fruit and vegetable harvesting. These crops require hand picking for quality reasons, and have a very high per-acre cost, as well as return. North Carolina, for instance, raises a variety of these horticultural crops—strawberries, blueberries, cucumbers, potatoes, and so on. Migratory labor has traditionally been used to harvest these crops. However, very little migratory labor had been used in tobacco harvesting, even though tobacco shares many of the characteristics of these horticultural crops: labor-intensive harvest and quality control problems, for example. During the 1970s, certain areas started using migrant labor for the tobacco harvest. Despite the concern in 1972, nonfarm employment and out-migration of rural labor had reduced the size of certain local labor markets. Some larger operations that had been organized by the lease and transfer mechanism now had to turn to outside sources of labor. Now, it is common to see migrant laborers working in tobacco, whether or not machine harvesting is being used.

Alternatives to Tobacco

Since the largest and most visible group of people who would be affected by a sharp change in demand for tobacco are farmers, some groups have tried to suggest alternative crops for tobacco farmers. Others have proposed the use of tobacco as a source of pure protein. Small farmers are usually the focus of this attention. Of course, nonfarm employment is the alternative that will be taken by most small farmers.

In much of the burley area, and in the piedmont areas of flue-cured, the tobacco allotments are small, and tobacco income is often already an income supplement to off-farm work. This phenomenon is especially true in the more urbanized parts of these regions. Jobs are more plentiful, and wages are higher than in more rural areas. This not only raises the opportunity cost of the growers' labor in pro-

ducing tobacco, but that of any hired labor also. Thus, tobacco growing is less profitable than it is in the more mechanized, larger units of
the eastern areas of North Carolina, South Carolina, and Georgia. If
it were not for the within county provisions of the lease and transfer
program, many producing units in the more urbanized areas would
have been out of business by now.

If the tobacco support program dies, off-farm employment will
be chosen by many in even the more profitable areas. It was noted
earlier that harvest labor released by mechanization was readily ab-
sorbed into nonfarming pursuits. This process should continue as it
has in times past and in other places.

Some groups and individuals feel that off-farm work, either in
one's own area or at a more distant location, is not the preferred solution to the displaced labor problem (see Adams in Finger 1981).
These people believe that there ought to be on-farm opportunities
for anyone who chooses that way of life, no matter what the resource
base available. They see small farmers as a desirable part of society.
This view is a philosophical position, and not really amenable to economic analysis. Yet economic analysis can shed some light on their
predictions of income and survival.

Their basic premise is probably correct: Small tobacco farmers
are the least likely to survive a process that reduces the profitability
of growing tobacco. The next step would be to find an alternative
enterprise on the farm that could replace tobacco and allow small
producers to remain on the farm. Agriculturalists divide crops into
two categories—field crops and horticultural crops. Field crops are
the extensive, machinery-intensive crops such as corn, wheat, and
soybeans. Horticultural crops are fruits, vegetables, and tree crops.
In general, horticultural crops are labor intensive with high per-acre
returns. Field crops have low returns per acre but can be grown on a
much larger scale. Tobacco, as we have seen, shares many characteristics with the horticultural crops. The returns per acre are high, the
labor requirements per acre are high, and hand labor is necessary for
certain operations for quality control purposes. If one just examines
the size and labor requirements of the operation, it appears that a
transition to some horticultural crop might be easy. Things are not
that simple, however.

There is a tendency to look at farm enterprise budgets, calculate net returns per acre, and then point out that resources could be devoted to growing strawberries, apples, or tomatoes, which in some years have a higher return per acre than tobacco. These are all specialty crops that require knowledge of production techniques. Human capital that is specific to growing tobacco is simply not transferable to growing strawberries. The basic question, of course, is why are these small tobacco farmers not now growing these vegetable crops if that would be more profitable than tobacco? While entry into tobacco production is restricted, entry into these other enterprises is not. The answer to the question is that resource allocations have been made on the basis of risk, as well as other considerations. Even if irrigation lowers weather and yield risks, the price risk is always present. Alternative crops may be an option to some tobacco farmers, but they will not be the salvation for all, if the program were to go.

Another alternative that has been proposed for tobacco growers is to continue to grow the product but to make the end use protein rather than smoking tobacco. Protein is one of the basic necessities of human and animal diets. All living matter, including tobacco, has protein in its makeup. Diets of people with higher incomes may contain a large amount of animal protein from meat and dairy products. Diets of those with lower incomes derive their protein primarily from plants. Beans and rice, for instance, a diet in parts of Latin America, provide all the essential amino acids of protein necessary for a human diet. Soybeans are a rich source of protein; a protein supplement can be derived from the bean to be added to other foods or processed directly. Researchers have found that protein extraction from tobacco leaves is a viable process. So far only laboratory experiments have been conducted, and there is no evidence that tobacco protein is cost effective on a commercial scale when compared to other sources of plant protein.

6
INTERNATIONAL TRADE IN TOBACCO

Introduction

Tobacco has been an important export crop since colonial days. The value of tobacco exports currently is over 7 percent of the value of all agricultural commodities exported. Since the value of tobacco produced is only 4 percent or so of the total value of all agricultural output in the United States, a minor crop on a national scale is a major export crop from this country. Currently, imports of unmanufactured tobacco are an issue in the tobacco industry, although we have historically imported tobacco in various forms. Table 6.1 presents historical data on tobacco exports from the United States. More recent data from the post-World War II period are contained in

TABLE 6.1
Exports of Unmanufactured Tobacco, Selected Years 1790–1930

Year	Quantity (millions pounds)	Value (millions dollars)
1790	118	4
1800	79	NA
1810	84	5
1820	84	8
1830	84	6
1840	119	10
1850	146	10
1860	167	16
1870	186	21
1880	216	16
1890	244	21
1900	335	29
1910	353	38
1920	468	245
1930	561	145

Source: U.S. Department of Commerce, Bureau of the Census, 1960

Table 6.2. Tables 6.3 and 6.4 present the recent history of U.S. production and export of tobacco as it compares to these measures worldwide.

The more recent data yield some insight into the current policy problems surrounding tobacco. At the end of World War II the U.S. share of world exports of flue-cured tobacco was over 60 percent. By 1980, that share was down to 29 percent. The actual level of exports was not declining so much; the amount that competitors were exporting to a growing market was increasing. This maintenance of the level of U.S. exports is really quite amazing. Through the operation of the support price program, the price of U.S. tobacco relative to competing tobaccos was quite high. In 1965, the net export price of U.S. flue-cured tobacco was approximately twice that of (then) Rhodesian tobacco, which was generally acknowledged to be the next highest quality tobacco, after the United States. The implication of the observed prices is that the U.S. has substantial market power in

TABLE 6.2
Exports by Type of Tobacco, 1956–80

Year	Type 11–14 Flue-Cured (1,000 pounds)	Type 21–23 Fire-Cured (1,000 pounds)	Type 31 Burley (1,000 pounds)
1956	465,070	30,268	28,224
1957	441,461	24,180	28,057
1958	442,682	24,947	34,779
1959	419,213	24,016	36,347
1960	474,630	27,211	41,327
1961	485,452	34,898	45,171
1962	430,940	23,640	53,461
1963	498,368	28,312	57,425
1964	444,063	27,289	55,654
1965	423,116	32,858	57,128
1966	587,116	31,003	57,277
1967	533,261	33,785	53,376
1968	525,285	24,299	54,923
1969	534,636	29,555	58,118
1970	533,998	32,971	54,414
1971	480,039	22,139	54,729
1972	518,810	26,363	75,616
1973	598,048	28,661	86,759
1974	548,293	20,791	67,902
1975	522,454	21,927	92,422
1976	514,228	27,503	116,835
1977	539,069	20,433	116,489
1978	598,669	25,820	121,471
1979	520,000	22,463	133,283
1980	490,000	19,865	105,494

Source: U.S. Department of Agriculture. Various years. *Annual Report of To-bacco Statistics*

flue-cured tobacco, which stems largely from quality. The welfare aspect of this power is analyzed in Chapter 3. Here, the concept of product differentiation in this kind of market is described, a model useful for analyzing such markets is presented, and some analysis of the flue-cured tobacco market is done.

TABLE 6.3
United States and World Production of Flue-Cured and Burley Tobacco

Year	Flue-Cured			Burley		
	United States (million pounds)	World (million pounds)	U.S. as Percent of total	United States (million pounds)	World (million pounds)	U.S. as Percent of total
1955–59 Avg.	1,208	2,914	41	486	595	82
1960–64 Avg.	1,336	3,302	40	624	778	80
1965–69 Avg.	1,093	3,666	30	574	824	70
1970	1,193	3,937	30	561	906	62
1971	1,078	3,918	28	473	868	55
1972	1,012	4,076	25	601	1,094	55
1973	1,157	4,404	27	450	944	48
1974	1,241	4,788	26	613	1,113	55
1975	1,415	5,100	28	639	1,240	52
1976	1,316	5,021	26	679	1,283	53
1977	1,130	5,816	19	617	1,276	48
1978	1,232	6,239	20	626	1,311	48
1979	946	5,455	17	446	1,232	36
1980	1,086	5,315	20	558	1,256	45
1981	1,144	6,507	18	716	1,408	52
1982	994	7,516	13	773	1,586	49

Source: U.S. Department of Agriculture. Various years. *Annual Report of Tobacco Statistics*

TABLE 6.4
United States and World Exports of Flue-Cured and Burley Tobacco

Year	Flue-Cured			Burley		
	United States (million pounds)	World (million pounds)	U.S. as Percent of total	United States (million pounds)	World (million pounds)	U.S. as Percent of total
1955–59 Avg.	413	683	60	28	47	60
1960–64 Avg.	397	772	52	42	74	57
1965–69 Avg.	415	790	53	46	106	44
1970	368	797	46	41	125	33
1971	342	831	41	36	128	28
1972	425	1,046	41	54	175	31
1973	418	1,088	38	59	210	28
1974	441	1,232	36	61	265	23
1975	391	1,176	33	62	231	27
1976	379	1,208	31	68	258	26
1977	412	1,238	33	79	291	27
1978	455	1,366	33	91	319	29
1979	371	1,236	30	82	313	26
1980	391	1,326	29	91	342	27
1981	386	1,510	26	72	343	21

Source: U.S. Department of Agriculture. Various years. *Annual Report of Tobacco Statistics*

Product Differentiation in Tobacco

This ability to continue exports when our price is higher than our competitors' means that foreign consumers view U.S. tobacco as a different product from tobacco from Brazil, Zimbabwe, or elsewhere. In a series of papers beginning in 1969, Paul Armington formalized this concept into "a theory of demand for products distinguished by place of production" (Armington, 1969a, 1969b). In 1978 several researchers at North Carolina State University used this model to examine individual commodities (Grennes, Johnson, and Thursby 1978). Previously, the model had been used to deal with more aggregate products. Agricultural goods were thought to be homogeneous, and more than one price could not prevail. We showed in the last-cited work that even for a good as seemingly homogeneous as wheat, it could prove useful to view that good as heterogeneous. In some earlier work, it had been shown that for several agricultural commodities market shares did not go to zero or one if the price in one country deviated from prices in other countries (Johnson 1971).

Why do we observe different prices for what appears to be the same product? When the good is traded internationally, there are essentially two reasons why goods may be differentiated by place of origin. One has to do with features of the good. One view of demand theory is that consumers ultimately desire product characteristics, and products can combine these characteristics in different proportions. In the case of wheat, for instance, a desired characteristic is protein and different wheats have different protein contents. We have seen that there are many varieties of tobacco, and the final product, such as cigarettes, may be a blend of several varieties. Even in the case of a single variety such as flue-cured, there are clear quality differences between tobacco grown in different countries.

Quality is difficult to identify objectively for tobacco. For purposes of the price support programs, government graders utilize over 150 grades for flue-cured tobacco alone. This grade determines the support price that each pile of tobacco will receive on the warehouse floor. These grades were discussed and listed in Chapter 3. The criteria that are used for these grades are: stalk position, color, texture, cleanliness, and the grader's judgment of the level of quality for a given set of other factors. Such a grade is obviously not a perfect measure of the quality of leaf in a particular pile. It is common knowledge that cigarette manufacturers use many fewer grades than do the government graders. Since they are going to blend the tobacco for the final product, their buyers can aggregate many government grades into a single company requirement.

At one time, the present author had access to a sample of observations on purchases of tobacco by Imperial Tobacco Company, which included the government grade and then certain measurable attributes of that tobacco, such as nicotine, sugar, and so on. I then tried to form a hedonic price index where the price of the tobacco was related to the measurable factors. In principle, if the analysis were successful, one would be able implicitly to price the factors. One would then have a measure of how much a unit of a factor contributed to price changes. Unfortunately, the analysis was unsuccessful, in the sense that the factors explained so little of the variation in price that the results had little meaning. Since all data of this kind are proprietary, no public analysis of quality is available.

While quality may not be objective to an outside observer, it certainly exists. Apparently, one can take the same varieties of tobacco grown in the flue-cured belts of the United States, transfer them elsewhere in the world, and the tobacco will be noticeably different to cigarette manufacturers and smokers. This is the distinction by place of origin that is important. The quality superiority of U.S. tobacco essentially has to do with flavor, mildness, and texture. Up until a few years ago smokers in the United Kingdom preferred a 100 percent Virginia (their term for flue-cured) cigarette. They represented a strong market for U.S. leaf. Imperial Tobacco Company, a British firm, employed buyers and maintained processing facilities in this country. Then Great Britain entered the European Economic Community (EEC); the relative price of U.S. leaf kept rising as more foreign sources entered the EEC, and Imperial reduced its volume of imports and shut down their U.S. facilities.

The second way in which goods may be differentiated has to do with the characteristics of the supplier (or buyer) rather than the good. Such things as custom and language may bind trading partners, as some transactions' costs are thereby reduced. The overall reliability of a supplier, or market services, such as credit terms, may affect observed prices. Long-term contracts may also keep a trade flow going despite a perceived price difference. This last effect probably entered into Imperial's decision to keep their U.S. processing facilities open as long as they did, but it was clearly the quality difference that led them to establish such facilities in the first place.

In the economics literature, a related concept to the differentiated goods model is that of intraindustry trade (Grubel and Lloyd 1975). If one does not a priori expect to observe different prices for the same good, neither does one expect a country both to import and export the same commodity. That is, the economic theory that is used to explain international trade usually deals, at the elementary level at least, with export goods, import goods, and nontraded goods. In the typical two country model, one country exports X and the other country imports it; the roles are then reversed for Y. When one goes to the data, however, things are not so simple. Countries are observed both importing and exporting the same good. At the highest level of aggregation these observations are understandable; an electrical machinery category, for instance, may include many individual products. The problem is not simply one of aggregation, however. Simultaneous importing and exporting of the same good is observed at the smallest levels of aggregation. There are some explanations of this phenomenon that are not relevant to tobacco, but one that is relevant is the same issue discussed above, namely, product differentiation.

The quantity of flue-cured and burley tobacco imported into the United States has risen sharply since 1975, as shown in Tables 6.5 and 6.6. The United States has imported some tobacco throughout this century, especially Turkish or Oriental tobacco. This type of tobacco is used as a flavoring agent in cigarettes and has never been grown successfully in this country. A natural question to ask is, why have imports of flue-cured and burley tobacco risen so much?

The basic explanation for the import increase is the quality problem. As noted previously, the quality of tobacco varies by leaf position on the stalk. The lowest leaves are the poorest in quality, and thus command the lowest price. Under the support program, however, they also have a minimum price. The basic technique of establishing support prices for various grades is that an average per-pound

TABLE 6.5
Imports and Domestic Use of Flue-Cured Tobacco 1969–81

Year	Imports	Domestic Disappearance (million pounds)	Total Use	Imports Share of Total (percent)
1969	5.7	645.9	651.6	0.9
1970	10.6	640.1	650.7	1.6
1971	11.2	662.5	673.7	1.7
1972	12.7	664.2	676.9	1.9
1973	20.4	703.4	723.4	2.8
1974	23.1	652.3	675.4	3.4
1975	24.4	670.6	695.0	3.5
1976	30.8	634.0	644.8	4.6
1977	55.0	608.2	663.2	8.3
1978	60.1	584.1	644.2	9.3
1979	84.8	563.1	647.9	13.1
1980	72.7	529.4	602.1	11.7
1981	63.3	488.8	552.1	11.5

Source: U.S. Department of Agriculture. Various years. *Annual Report of Tobacco Statistics*

price is established, following which the other grades are priced so that a weighted average of those grade prices is equal to the average price established by the formula. The highest price grades are those that have traditionally received a premium, and have been the differentiated product considered superior abroad. In recent years, as the formula called for high nominal prices, even this tobacco has been viewed as too high-priced abroad. Changes in grade structure over time have prevented too high a price for the best tobacco by compressing the distribution of support prices by grade. This means that the highest-priced tobacco increases less, but the lowest-priced tobacco increases more in order to achieve the same average target. Thus, domestic cigarette manufacturers may be paying relatively less for the superior tobaccos but they are paying relatively more for the low quality tobacco.

At the same time this pricing change was taking place tobacco had been made a commodity whose tariff structure was subject to

TABLE 6.6
Imports and Domestic Use of Burley Tobacco 1969–81

Year	Imports	Domestic Disappearance (million pounds)	Total Use	Imports Share of Total (percent)
1969	3.3	507.1	510.4	0.6
1970	3.2	503.0	506.2	0.6
1971	4.6	515.2	519.8	0.9
1972	8.9	534.5	543.4	1.6
1973	30.7	533.1	563.8	5.4
1974	47.7	518.8	566.5	8.4
1975	46.7	510.1	556.8	8.4
1976	37.9	489.6	527.5	7.2
1977	85.4	494.8	580.2	14.7
1978	89.1	502.8	591.9	15.1
1979	113.6	498.5	612.1	18.6
1980	136.9	477.6	614.5	22.3
1981	109.7	463.9	573.6	19.1

Source: U.S. Department of Agriculture. Various years. *Annual Report of Tobacco Statistics*

negotiations of the General Agreement on Tariffs and Trade (GATT). The U.S. tariff on smoking grade leaf was negotiated down. Even though only the first step has taken place, the general direction is down. Also, as has been previously noted, the quality of tobacco from Brazil and other places had improved. A clear incentive arose to substitute foreign tobacco for downstalk flue-cured tobacco, as the foreign tobacco had become as cheap as the domestic. The actual usage of these imports is not known, since it is proprietary information. Clearly, however, increased imports is one factor putting pressure on the support price program, and was discussed further in Chapter 3.

Another aspect of the import concern has to do with tariff give-back provisions. Under existing rules, a manufacturer who imports a raw material that has a tariff imposed on it can get the tariff proceeds back if the firm later exports a commodity that incorporates the

TABLE 6.7
U. S. Exports of Cigarettes by Year

Year	Million Cigarettes
1964	25,144
1965	23,050
1966	23,458
1967	23,651
1968	26,461
1969	24,970
1970	29,135
1971	31,812
1972	34,602
1973	41,543
1974	46,901
1975	49,935
1976	61,370
1977	66,845
1978	74,359
1979	79,717
1980	81,998
1981	82,582

Source: U.S. Department of Agriculture. Various years. *Annual Report of Tobacco Statistics.*

taxed raw material. That is, a cigarette manufacturer who exports cigarettes will be forgiven the tariff paid on unmanufactured tobacco used in those cigarettes. Cigarette manufacturers, then, do not have to be concerned about tariffs on imported tobacco to the extent they are also exporting cigarettes.

Table 6.7 shows the export of U.S. cigarettes from 1964 to 1981. In the early years of the series there is no pronounced trend, but starting in the early 1970s there is a pronounced upward trend. The quantity exported increases every year. By 1981 the quantity exported was more than three times that in the mid-1960s. This almost exactly matches the trend in imports of both flue-cured and burley. These series would indicate that little or no tariff was being paid by cigarette manufacturers who were simultaneously importing tobacco and exporting cigarettes. The 80 billion cigarettes utilize about 60 million pounds of flue-cured and about 50 million pounds of burley. Recent imports of burley have been more than the amount used in exported cigarettes, but the flue-cured imports have not been much more than the required amount.

These data present a puzzle to an analyst. Without more information, most of it proprietary, it is difficult to find causal relationships for these quite striking trends.

While the volume of U.S. tobacco exported has not changed much in the last 20 years, the identification and location of the customers have. In 1966 Great Britain imported about 120 million pounds of U.S. flue-cured tobacco, while in 1981 it imported about 30 million pounds. On the other hand, Spain imported 1.6 million pounds of flue-cured in 1965 and 28 million pounds in 1981. These and other changes are shown in Table 6.8. Japan, which was our third or fourth largest customer in the mid 1960s is currently our best customer.

Some of these changes have been the result of exogenous forces. Great Britain joined the Common Market in the early 1970s. As a result, the source of many of her imports changed. Britain came under the EEC tariff structure. This structure has a lower (or no) tariff on tobacco from certain other suppliers, so Britain has gone to other sources for much of her tobacco. In 1979 sanctions were lifted from tobacco from Zimbabwe, and this opened another lower cost source for Britain. The other EEC countries in the table, West Germany, Netherlands, and Belgium, also have downward trends, although not as pronounced as Britain's. Presumably, these trends are also due to the EEC tariff structure.

All countries tax tobacco products internally, and most countries collect taxes on imports through tariffs. Two countries, Japan and Sweden, collect their taxes in a different way. Each has established a governmental purchasing monopoly. Tobacco from the United States can enter duty free, but as a monopoly, the buying agency can charge whatever internal price it wishes, producing revenue in that way.

TABLE 6.8
U.S. Exports of Flue-Cured Tobacco to Selected Countries (1,000 pounds)

Year	Gt. Britain	W. Germany	Japan	Sweden	Spain	Netherlands	Belgium
1965	79,607	65,612	42,037	7,474	1,657	23,149	11,229
1966	119,076	106,289	40,504	10,033	4,197	22,025	16,451
1967	120,885	67,488	34,993	8,425	3,040	27,145	14,166
1968	96,635	89,967	31,106	6,916	4,187	24,049	13,473
1969	111,291	67,835	39,114	6,886	2,996	17,868	9,851
1970	95,141	88,961	41,215	9,792	5,093	15,617	11,683
1971	73,301	80,882	13,418	7,280	5,093	15,192	11,267
1972	89,800	75,507	66,082	8,400	4,214	11,688	8,993
1973	95,285	74,519	55,260	8,127	3,679	14,863	12,706
1974	71,463	71,289	77,107	6,659	7,484	14,125	10,247
1975	60,034	72,819	55,141	9,043	8,847	16,504	5,265
1976	51,247	50,133	90,389	7,145	0	13,747	4,943
1977	34,339	56,751	93,823	6,257	4,246	15,234	6,493
1978	108,805	35,393	72,600	8,609	17,363	14,577	11,951
1979	51,563	42,403	66,279	7,551	675	14,691	3,556
1980	24,899	63,087	52,677	7,551	23,177	24,343	4,484
1981	30,296	51,175	73,700	4,131	28,087	16,307	6,109

Source: U.S. Department of Agriculture. Various years. *Annual Report of Tobacco Statistics*

Some countries have nontariff barriers as well as tariff barriers against U.S. tobacco. Australia, for instance, has a mixing regulation; cigarettes manufactured in Australia have to contain a certain fraction of Australian-grown tobacco. In general, most U.S. tobacco exports go to developed countries with relatively stable policies. Tobacco was included in the Tokyo round of negotiation of the General Agreement on Tariffs and Trade. The tariffs were negotiated downward so that U.S. tariffs on imports, as well as foreign tariffs on U.S. tobaccco will go down in stages.

In considering the reduced market share for U.S. tobacco, domestic producers and other groups have expressed concern that competitors were subsidizing exports. This may be true for some countries at some times. Canada, for instance, has subsidized the export of flue-cured tobacco, but she does the same for other agricultural products. The institutions that Canada uses for these purposes are of long standing, and probably are not a very large factor in the declining U.S. share. Unfortunately, data and information are difficult to come by on this issue for countries like Brazil, whose market share has increased markedly in recent years. Most developing countries, like Brazil and South Korea, are intervening in their agricultural and/or export markets. Finding the cost of production in these competitor's markets would require more time than is warranted by the present study.

A Trade Model for Tobacco

The model used here divides the world into seven endogenous regions and an exogenous rest of the world (ROW). The seven include five major exporters (United States, Turkey, Greece, India, and Brazil), and two major importers (Japan, EEC).

The three basic assumptions underlying the model are:

1. The marginal rate of substitution between any two kinds of a good is independent of any other goods in the consumer's market basket.
2. The elasticity of substitution between any two kinds of a good in a given market is a constant.

3. The elasticity of substitution between any two kinds of a good in a given market equals the elasticity of substitution between any other kinds of the good in the same market.

Demand

The demand for any particular flow can be stated as:*

$$DIJ = EXIJ \neq \eta_{ijj} \, DPIJ + \sum_{\substack{h \neq j}}^{n-1} \eta_{ijh} \, DPIH + \sum_{k=1}^{m} \eta_{iwk} \, DPIK \quad (1)$$

where
    DIJ = percentage change in quantity of country J's tobacco going to country I,
    $EXIJ$ = percentage change in country I's, expenditure on country J's tobacco (taken as exogenous),
    $DPIJ$ = percentage change in the price of country J's tobacco in country I,
    η_{ijh} = price elasticity of demand for country J's tobacco with respect to the price of country H's tobacco in country I,
    η_{iwk} = price elasticity of demand for tobacco with respect to the price of good k in country I.

There are potentially n^2 of these equations; seven endogenous countries (regions) are specified. If all flows exist, there would be n^2 direct elasticities of the form η_{ijj} where the country of the last subscript is the same as the second, that is, the price of concern is the same as the tobacco being supplied. In addition, there would be $n^2(n - 1)$ cross elasticities for various kinds of tobacco.

The Armington-type restrictions greatly reduce the number of parameters involved. These restrictions allow one to generate all the necessary parameters from $2n$ basic parameters. The required pa-

---

*Note that the variables in these demand equations are stated in terms of percentage changes. They could just as easily be stated in terms of levels with the same parameters (elasticities). Absolute values of levels can easily be recaptured from knowledge of changes, and there are some computational and interpretative advantages to formulating the equations as changes.

rameters are a basic price elasticity for all tobacco in each region, and an elasticity of substitution for each region. The individual demand elasticities are then found as follows:

$$\eta_{ijj} = (-1)[(1 - s^i_j)\sigma^i + s^i_j(\eta^i)] \tag{2}$$

and

$$\eta_{ijk} = s^i_j[\sigma^i - \eta^i] \tag{3}$$

where the η_{ijj} and η_{ijh} have previously been defined, and σ^i is the elasticity of substitution in market i, η^i is the basic demand elasticity in market i, and s^i_j is the share of J's tobacco in market i, and all elasticities are given positive signs for convenience.

Supply

A model of the kind being considered would in general include n endogenous quantity supplied variables. These variables would be functions of domestic supply prices and various exogenous supply shifters. Total supply to the market of a particular tobacco (TSJ) is the sum of production (SJ) and net sales from inventories (NJ). Both of these sources are determined outside the model, so the total supplies of each of the seven regions (DTSJ's) are exogenous variables.

Price Equations

The model includes n^2 price equations of the form:

$$DPIJ = SPJ + LIJ \tag{4}$$

where SPJ is the change in the supply price in country J and the LIJ are exogenous shifters.

An equation such as (4) says that the change in the consumer price in I for a flow from J is equal to the change in the producer price in J plus any change in the margin between these two prices. It is here that changes in freight rates or other transportation costs, tariff, or other tax (or subsidy) changes can be entered.

Since it can be said that the exogenous shocks "drive" the model, the LIJ terms are crucial in predicting changes. Of course, their impact is only determined when the model is solved for the endogenous variables.

Equilibrium Conditions

There are n market clearing conditions that close the model. Since the model is specified in changes in variables, these equations state that the changes in demand for a particular country must equal the changes in quantity supplied by that country. Thus:

$$DTSJ = \sum_{I=1}^{n} \left(\frac{IJ}{J}\right)DIJ \tag{5}$$

where $\left(\frac{IJ}{J}\right)$ is the proportion of J's tobacco that goes to country I. If these proportions stay the same through time, this model belongs to the class of models that have become known as constant market share models.

Since the model consists of 7 endogenous regions, it potentially consists of $n^2 = 49$ demand equations, $n^2 = 49$ price equations, and $n = 7$ market clearing equations. Empirical considerations simplify the model, however, since 30 of the 49 potential trade flows are zero or negligible. This reduces the number of endogenous variables from $49 + 49 + 7 = 106$ to $19 + 19 + 7 = 45$.

Government Policy

The exogenous shifters that affect the demand side, income, prices of competing goods, and quantifiable health variables, are apt to be fairly predictable in terms of being on a trend. The real usefulness of the model for our work on grain was in analyzing government policies. Changes in policies such as trade controls and exchange rates enter through the LIJs in the price equation. That is, they are treated just like changes in transport costs and other cost changes. Other governmental policy changes can enter through the exogenous supply changes.

Excluding purely domestic flows, the model contains twelve price equations which link exporters and importers. For instance, for U.S. exports:

$$DPEU = SPU + LEU \tag{6}$$

$$DPJU = SPU + LJU \tag{7}$$

The demand price is expressed in the currency of the importing country, but the supply price is denominated in the currency of the exporting country. All prices are real prices, so that the inflation rate of the exporting country must be entered as one of the LIJs. For example, an X percent revaluation of the yen (equals devaluation of the dollar) will, for a given dollar price of U.S. tobacco, lower the yen price of U.S. tobacco by X percent. For a given exchange rate, an X percent inflation in the United States will raise the yen price of U.S. tobacco by X percent. Thus, a combination of an X percent U.S. inflation and an X percent U.S. devaluation will leave the yen price of U.S. tobacco unchanged. Exchange rate changes that are purely monetary in the sense of following purchasing power parity considerations do not affect the model. Currency changes caused by real forces (cost, demand, capital flows) do alter relative prices and the structure of trade. Notice also that an X percent of U.S. export subsidy (tax) to Japan has the same effect on prices and trade as an X percent import subsidy (tariff) in Japan or an X percent reduction in transport costs between the United States and Japan. Thus, the model abstracts from the questions of who receives the tariff revenue, raises the revenue for a subsidy, or receives transport revenue. Similarly in trade relations with ROW, the model does not distinguish between commercial sales or gifts.

Some Examples

The calculations used in this section are based on a set of elasticities that have the demand elasticity inside each country at $-.2$, and the elasticity of substitution among tobaccos as 3.0. From these values and information on market shares the array of elasticities in Tables 6.9 and 6.10 can be derived.

TABLE 6.9
Direct Price Elasticities of Demand for Unmanufactured Tobacco ($\eta_{iij} = (-1)[(1 - S_j^i) \sigma^i + S_j^i (\eta^i)]$ with $\sigma = 3.0, \eta = .2$)

Consumer	United States	Turkey	Greece	India	Brazil	EEC	Japan
United States	-.656	-2.807	-2.947	—	-2.978	—	—
Turkey	—	-.200	—	—	—	—	—
Greece	-2.980	—	-.220	—	—	—	—
India	—	—	—	-.200	—	—	—
Brazil	—	—	—	—	-.200	—	—
EEC	-2.297	-2.882	-2.852	-2.877	-2.857	-2.479	—
Japan	-2.698	-2.955	-2.947	-2.958	—	—	.729

Source: Compiled by the author

115

TABLE 6.10

Cross Price Elasticities of Demand for Unmanufactured Tobacco ($\eta_{ijh} = S_j^i [\sigma^i - \eta^i]$ with $\sigma = 3.0$, $\eta = .2$)

Consumer	United States	Turkey	Greece	India	Brazil	EEC	Japan
United States	2.344	.193	.053	—	.022	—	—
Turkey	—	2.800	—	—	—	—	—
Greece	.020	—	2.780	—	—	—	—
India	—	—	—	2.800	—	—	—
Brazil	—	—	—	—	2.800	—	—
EEC	.703	.118	.148	.123	.143	.521	—
Japan	.302	.045	.053	.042	—	—	2.271

Source: Compiled by the author

At this point it is easier to think of the model as having the following structure: The 45 endogenous variables are a vector Y; the demand parameters and other coefficients on variables are the 45×45 matrix X, and the exogenous shifters are a 45×1 vector A.* The solution for the endogenous variable is:

$$Y = X^{-1}A \qquad (8)$$

Now we can either use all of the information available and calculate the vector Y, or, if interest centers on particular variables, we can isolate those and examine them. For the numerical calculations, the market share data represent a rough average for the 1970s. The variables and the exogenous changes are percentage changes. There are both theoretical and empirical advantages to expressing things this way.

Table 6.11 shows two rows from X^{-1}, row one for U.S. consumption of its own tobacco, and row 20, U.S. price of its own tobacco. If one wanted to forecast next year's domestic consumption of U.S. tobacco, one would put in known or forecast changes in the exogenous shifters in A, multiply each change in A by the multiplier shown in the column, add them up, and the result would be DUU. Alternatively, one can ask partial equilibrium questions by isolating particular exogenous changes, assigning others the value zero, thus holding them constant. For example, holding everything constant but real income, a 1 percent increase in income in the United States would lead to a .5 percent change in consumption. This is shown by the element in Table 6.11, column 1, .541. That is, holding everything else constant, a change in income in the United States, after allowing for the general equilibrium effects inherent in the model, has an impact multiplier effect of .541. The large multipliers on U.S. own flow are income and change in supply. The next biggest one is a change in cost (transport, exchange rate, and so on) between Europe and the United States. Domestic policy is not being considered at the moment, so the $-.263$ for the U.S. own price is multiplied by zero and can be ignored.

---

*Actually the dimension of the problem is 51×51, since it is necessary to include 6 identities for exports to ROW in the solution.

TABLE 6.11
Impact Multipliers for U.S. Own Consumption and U.S.
Internal Price from Various Exogenous Shifters

Endogenous	Exogenous	Multiplier for DUU	Multiplier for DPUU
DUU	Y, P	.541	1.156
DEU		−.108	.271
DJU		−.019	.048
DTT		.028	.094
DET		.010	.033
DJT		.002	.006
DUT		.019	.064
DGG		.001	.025
DEG		.002	.033
DJG		.000	.005
DUG		.001	.013
DII		−.149	.176
DEI		−.004	.015
DJI		−.001	.003
DBB		−.006	.106
DEB		−.001	.024
DUB		−.000	.004
DEE		−.022	.082
DJJ		−.065	.220
DPUU		−.263	.534
DPEU	T, R, Z, X	.232	−.479
DPJU		.031	−.055
DPTT		−.003	−.009
DPET		−.044	−.042
DPJT		−.009	−.004
DPUT		.055	.055
DPGG		−.000	−.003
DPEG		−.024	−.029
DPJG		−.005	−.002
DPUG		.029	.030
DPIE		.005	−.018
DPEI		−.004	.014
DPJI		−.001	.004
DPBB		.001	−.011
DPEB		−.014	−.005

Table 6.11
(Continued)

Endogenous	Exogenous	Multiplier for DUU	Multiplier for DPUU
DPUB		.014	.016
DPEE		–0–	–0–
DPJJ		–0–	–0–
DSPU	S, I	.652	– 1.642
DSPT		– .066	– .223
DSPG		– .005	– .102
DSPI		.058	– .211
DSPB		.009	– .151
DSPE		.029	– .108
DSPJ		.065	– .220
DRU	DR	– .066	.167
DRT		.008	.027
DRG		.001	.027
DRI		– .005	.017
DRB		– .001	.016
DRE		– .007	.026

Y, P = Income, other prices; T, R, Z = Transport costs, X = exchange rate, Z = other policies and wedges; S, I = Changes in supply, Inventory changes; DR = Change in ROW exports.
Source: Compiled by the author

The price side of the picture is, in a way, more interesting, and more illustrative of the effect of the general equilibrium nature of the model. Consider the block of shifters in rows 39–45. The biggest multiplier, of course, is associated with a change in U.S. supply, but changes in supply elsewhere are not negligible. The U.S. own multiplier can be interpreted as the partial derivative of internal price with respect to an exogenous change in supply. A 1 percent decrease in U.S. supply, then, is associated with a 1.6 percent increase in the internal price, all other variables being held constant. Thus, if domestic production were cut 10% through a policy change, the forecast for this model would be for a 16% increase in price.

Changes in output for countries that are being treated as exogenous for this problem can be handled as if they were changes in exports to ROW. A 10 percent decrease in shipments to ROW is associated with a 1.67 percent decrease in the U.S. internal price.

One forecast of considerable interest from this model is that resulting from an exogenous shift in the column for DPEU. The multiplier here is for a change in tariff, transport cost, and so on, between the United States and the EEC. A 10 percent increase in the EEC tariff, for instance, is accompanied by a 4.8 percent decrease in the U.S. price. In the case of Japan, which in the 1970s was a smaller customer, the effect of an increased tariff is almost negligible on U.S. price. A 10 percent change there is accompanied by a one-half of one percent change in the U.S. price.

The Elasticity of Demand for Tobacco

The general equilibrium model of the previous section yields plausible forecasts for various exogenous shocks. For some purposes, however, a partial equilibrium approach is sufficient. The welfare analysis of Chapter 3 is an example. For such an analysis of international trade, it is the excess demand and supply elasticities that are required. There are two ways to try to determine these elasticities—direct estimates by statistical inference, and construction from known or assumed parameters. Both of these methods were used in Chapter 3; the 1965 study used a constructed elasticity of demand, while the 1981 study used an estimated one.

The demand for tobacco is a derived demand from cigarettes and other tobacco products. There is, more or less, a consensus on the elasticity of demand for cigarettes. Most analyses have found elasticities below 1 in absolute value, and there is a striking clustering of estimates in the $-.4$ to $-.5$ range. The elasticity of demand for tobacco can be smaller or larger than that of cigarettes depending on substitution possibilities of inputs in cigarette making. A smaller elasticity seems more plausible, especially in the short run. A domestic elasticity of $-.2$ for tobacco has been used by several analysts (Johnson 1965; Seagraves 1983). A careful study by Norton (1981) estimated statistically an elasticity of $-.19$, so that one can have some confidence that $-.2$ is in the possible range. This elasticity is important in the construction of an excess demand elasticity.

The derivation of the formula for the excess demand facing a particular exporting country is well known. The quantity demanded from a country is the difference between the quantity demanded from the rest of the world and the quantity supplied by the rest of the world. In symbols:

$$X = D - S \tag{9}$$

If this expression is differentiated with respect to price and then the terms are converted to elasticities, one will get the following expression for the elasticity of demand for exports:

$$\eta_x = \frac{D}{X} \eta_w - \frac{S}{X} \epsilon_w \tag{10}$$

where η_x is the elasticity of demand for exports, η_w is the elasticity of demand in the rest of the world and ϵ_w is the elasticity of supply in the rest of the world. If the commodity is flue-cured tobacco from the United States, then the elasticity facing the United States depends not only on elasticities, but also on the U.S. market share in the world market. η_w is negative; the inverse shares are positive, as is ϵ_w. Therefore η_x is a negative number that is larger in absolute value than the domestic demand elasticity. The smaller the U.S. market share the larger the export demand elasticity will be.

In the 1965 study mentioned earlier, the following parameters were used: The domestic demand elasticity was taken as $-.2$; the domestic supply elasticity was taken as .2; D was 5.36; and S was 4.36. These numbers imply an elasticity in the neighborhood of -2.0. The domestic U.S. price was assumed to be 33 percent above the world price. An elasticity as low as 2.0 implies substantial market power for the United States. As we saw earlier, the United States has been employing its market power to collect rents from foreign consumers of U.S. tobacco. The United States, by this analysis, was not exploiting its monopoly power to the fullest extent, however.

Underlying the analysis of welfare gains from exploiting the less-than-perfectly elastic demand curve for exports is the concept of the optimum tariff, in this case, an optimum export tax. It should be noted that under the U.S. Constitution an export tax cannot be levied. The tobacco price support program, and other domestic price increasing devices, operate exactly as an export tax, however, although the tax proceeds are distributed in a presumably different fashion. How much a country can increase its price relative to the world price before the gains diminish rather than increase is a function of the demand elasticity the country faces. The rate for which the gains are a maximum is known as the optimum tariff. A well-known formula for this tariff is $1/\eta - 1$, where the absolute value of η is used. An elasticity of -2.0 implies an optimum tariff of 100 percent, which is considerably larger than the 33 percent that was estimated in the 1960s.

As we saw earlier, the U.S. market share has fallen steadily since about 1965. This decline is not a result of falling U.S. exports, but of competing suppliers increasing their exports. This decline makes the ratios D/X and S/X larger, making the calculated elasticity larger. Using the same formula for η_x, but using 1980 market share ratios, the implied elasticity of demand is in the neighborhood of -5.0 rather than -2.0. This means that the implied optimum tariff is much less, possibly 25 percent. Since the difference between the domestic U.S. price and the world price appears to be closer to 20 percent currently, the United States would appear to be using nearly all of its market power.

Statistical estimates of the export elasticities from time series data continue to yield smaller estimates than the constructed elasticities. Buccola and Richardson (1979) and Norton (1981) using differing techniques and different data both get estimates more in the neighborhood of -2.0. Norton applied three stage least squares estimating techniques to a three equation model of the U.S. flue-cured tobacco market. One of these equations was the foreign demand for U.S. tobacco. The long run demand elasticity was estimated to be -2.3, and was statistically significant at the 5 percent level.

Buccola and Richardson looked at three separate import markets, Great Britain, West Germany, and Japan; they also aggregated the United States and Canada into a "North American" tobacco. They used single equation techniques to estimate demand functions for each market separately. The elasticities for Japan, West Germany, and Great Britain are, respectively, -1.34, -1.68, and -1.91. These are all larger than one in absolute value and have the correct sign. They are only slightly smaller than Norton's figures.

How can we reconcile the discrepancy between these lower estimates and a constructed elasticity that appears to be growing with time? One part of the explanation, no doubt, has to do with the time series. The early years of both studies included observations when the elasticity may have been much smaller. Since a regression coefficient is in the nature of an average, an elasticity of -2.3 may simply be the correct estimate for that data. Another reason to believe that elasticities may not be as large as the currently constructed ones has to do with the constrained nature of the markets involved. As noted earlier, there is intervention in almost all tobacco import markets. Quantity responsiveness to price change may not be allowed to the extent that a totally free market would allow. State trading, mixing regulations, variable levies, and other devices can effectively make the price elasticity zero for certain quantities. The average elasticity across all of our export outlets may indeed be smaller than casual calculations would suggest.

7

TOBACCO AND THE FISC

Tobacco has always been a target for taxation, from British import duties in colonial days to today's federal and state excise taxes on cigarettes. Table 7.1 shows some historical data on tobacco excise taxes. Several interesting items can be found in the table. One, unrelated to tobacco per se, is how large a fraction of total tax receipts excise taxes were until World War I. In most years until 1910, customs duties were the biggest single source of government revenue. Tobacco excise taxes were not a very large item in total taxes from 1865 to 1920. They averaged about 10 percent of internal revenue collections for this period. That is not insignificant by any means, but it is not very great either.

The change in both tobacco excises and total collections between 1915 and 1920 is dramatic. Several things occurred at that

TABLE 7.1
U.S. Government Tax Collections, 1865–1950 (million dollars)

Year	Total	Internal Revenue	Customs	Tobacco Excise
1865	334	209	85	11
1870	411	185	180	31
1875	288	110	157	37
1880	834	124	187	39
1885	324	112	181	26
1890	403	143	230	34
1895	325	143	152	30
1900	567	295	233	59
1905	544	234	262	46
1910	676	290	334	58
1915	698	416	210	80
1920	6,695	5,405	323	296
1925	3,780	2,589	548	345
1930	4,178	3,039	587	450
1935	3,800	3,278	343	459
1940	5,983	5,303	349	609
1945	47,750	43,902	355	932
1950	41,311	39,449	423	1,328

Source: U.S. Department of Commerce, Bureau of the Census. 1960.

time. First, U.S. participation in World War I had increased the size of government substantially, so that receipts had to grow. The increase in tobacco excise taxes was the result of a new cigarette tax imposed in 1917. Note, however, that while tobacco excises increased almost fourfold as a result of the tax, these taxes as a fraction of the total fell sharply. In 1913, a constitutional amendment was ratified that allowed an income tax. From 1920 on, this tax would dwarf other federal revenue collection vehicles. Tobacco and cigarette taxes grew steadily, however, and by 1950 had reached a billion dollars in total.

Table 7.2 shows both federal and state tobacco excise tax collections since 1960. The first state excise tax on cigarettes was enacted by Iowa in 1921. Table 7.3 converts the tax receipts from Table 7.2 to constant 1967 dollars. There, the general downward trend in federal

TABLE 7.2
Tax Receipts from Cigarettes (million dollars)

Year	Federal	State
1960	1,864	923
1961	1,924	1,001
1962	1,957	1,074
1963	2,011	1,124
1964	1,977	1,196
1965	2,070	1,284
1966	2,006	1,541
1967	2,023	1,615
1968	2,066	1,884
1969	2,082	2,056
1970	2,036	2,308
1971	2,150	2,536
1972	2,151	2,831
1973	2,221	3,112
1974	2,383	3,250
1975	2,261	3,286
1976	2,435	3,462
1977	2,358	3,500
1978	2,408	3,653
1979	2,455	3,641
1980	2,403	3,738
1981	2,538	3,893

Source: U.S. Department of Agriculture. *Annual Reports of Tobacco Statistics.*

tax receipts can be seen. This effect was noted in Chapter 4, where it was pointed out that the fixed per-unit tax was actually lowering the real price of cigarettes. Table 7.4 shows the current level of taxation in each state, the year of the initial tax, and the date of the latest tax level. By the end of World War II, 30 states had enacted cigarette taxes. By 1960, all but two states were taxing cigarettes. In 1969, North Carolina initiated a 2 cents per-pack tax and made taxing of cigarettes unanimous among the states.

Note the range of tax rates. They range from the low of 2 cents per pack in North Carolina to 21 cents in Connecticut, Florida, and Massachusetts. The states with the lowest tax rates, North Carolina,

TABLE 7.3
Real Cigarette Taxes Since 1967 (million 1967 dollars)

Year	Federal	State
1967	2,023	1,615
1968	1,941	1,808
1969	1,896	1,872
1970	1,751	1,985
1971	1,772	2,091
1972	1,717	2,302
1973	1,669	2,338
1974	1,613	2,107
1975	1,403	2,038
1976	1,428	2,030
1977	1,293	1,928
1978	1,232	1,869
1979	1,129	1,701
1980	974	1,515
1981	932	1,429

Source: Compiled by the author from Table 7.2 and the Consumer Price Index.

Virginia, and Kentucky, are not only states with large acreages of tobacco, but they also have major tobacco manufacturing facilities.
South Carolina, a major tobacco producing state, has the next lowest
tax, but Tennessee has a tax of 13 cents, which is almost equal to the
50-state average of 13.36 cents. Cigarette manufacturing appears to
be the biggest factor in the taxing of cigarettes. These differentials in
taxing have caused some problems that will be discussed shortly, but
some inferences about the differentials may be made.

Different states use different revenue bases, of course. Some
states rely more on income taxes than excise taxes, for instance.
Some states rely more on local government taxes than others. But
neither of those observations explains the variability of the tax rates.
Consider another highly visible product that is also taxed in all 50
states—retail gasoline. In 1979, the range of per-gallon tax rates was
from 6 cents in Nevada to 12 cents in Washington, but there was only
one observation each for 6 and 12. The other 49 observations were
from 7 to 11 cents per gallon. The mean tax rate was 8.16 cents. The
range and variability of these state tax rates is much less than that for
cigarettes.

Both commodities are ideal tax sources. The tax is easily collect-ible at the point of sale; there is a federal excise tax on both com-modities, so that untaxed production and sale is virtually impossible; and both commodities have relatively inelastic demands so that short-run sales are not much affected by tax changes. The difference is that tobacco taxes, like liquor taxes, are partly sumptuary in na-ture. Cigarettes have a bad image. Smokers do not coalesce into strong pressure groups, so legislatures find cigarettes an easy com-modity to tax. In recent years, they have also found it easy to in-crease the tax. Each state is free to set the tax rate wherever it wishes. As a consequence, some states have set the rate at more than one third of the retail price of cigarettes.

This wide disparity in state tax rates led to a spate of illegal activ-ity in the late 1970s. There was a big upsurge in the interstate smug-gling of cigarettes. This activity had semicomic overtones in the press and came to be known as "buttlegging." Smuggling, of course, is an illegal transfer from the tax authorities to smugglers and con-sumers. In the case of domestic cigarettes these transfers were gener-ally nonviolent, and more often than not conducted in relatively small quantity. As the disparity in tax rates grew, so did the smuggling activity. To a large extent this was an east coast phenomenon: from the low-tax states of North Carolina and Virginia to New Jersey, Pennsylvania, New York, Connecticut, and Massachusetts, and from North Carolina to Florida. The tax authorities in the high-tax states were naturally unhappy. The sales in the low-tax states were not ille-gal, since the state and federal taxes were paid on these sales. That large sales of cigarettes were destined to be sent north was obvious to sellers and authorities in the low-tax states, but there was no compel-ling reason to halt the sales.

Authorities in the high-tax states found it difficult to enforce their tax laws with sufficient strength to slow the smuggling. A fed-eral statute prohibiting the smuggling was passed in 1980. This stat-ute had sufficient penalties to deter the activity. It was a relatively simple matter to pass such a statute. In our society no one can pub-licly support smuggling. Since the product smuggled had image problems, ending an illegal activity was especially popular.

The sale of cigarettes in low-tax states for consumption in high-tax states continues. There has been informal smuggling of this kind by individual consumers for a long time. Wherever the transporta-

TABLE 7.4
State Tax Rates on Cigarettes by State, January 1, 1982

State	Rate of Tax per Standard Package of 20 (cents)	Date of Present Rate	Year Tax Enacted	State	Rate of Tax per Standard Package of 20 (cents)	Date of Present Rate	Year Tax Enacted
Alabama	16	1980	1927	Montana	12	1971	1947
Alaska	8	1961	1949	Nebraska	14	1981	1947
Arizona	13	1974	1933	Nevada	10	1969	1947
Arkansas	17.75	1971	1925	New Hampshire	12	1975	1939
California	10	1967	1959	New Jersey	19	1972	1948
Colorado	10	1978	1964	New Mexico	12	1968	1943
Connecticut	21	1971	1935	New York	15	1972	1939
Delaware	14	1971	1949	North Carolina	2	1969	1969
Florida	21	1971	1943	North Dakota	12	1970	1925
Georgia	12	1971	1923	Ohio	14	1981	1931
Hawaii	17	1980	1939	Oklahoma	18	1979	1933
Idaho	9.1	1972	1945	Oregon	16	1981	1966
Illinois	12	1969	1941	Pennsylvania	18	1970	1935
Indiana	10.5	1965	1947	Rhode Island	18	1975	1939
Iowa	18	1981	1921	South Carolina	7	1977	1923
Kansas	11	1970	1927	South Dakota	15	1981	1923
Kentucky	3	1970	1936	Tennessee	13	1969	1925
Louisiana	11	1970	1926	Texas	18.5	1971	1931

State				State			
Maine	16	1974	1941	Utah	10	1979	1923
Maryland	13	1980	1958	Vermont	12	1969	1937
Massachusetts	21	1975	1939	Virginia	2.5	1966	1960
Michigan	11	1970	1947	Washington	20	1981	1935
Minnesota	18	1971	1947	West Virginia	17	1978	1947
Mississippi	11	1973	1930	Wisconsin	20	1981	1939
Missouri	9	1969	1956	Wyoming	8	1967	1951

Source: U.S. Department of Agriculture. 1982. *Annual Report of Tobacco Statistics.*

tion costs of crossing a border are less than the price differential, these sales will continue. There is less organized activity, but a large but unknown quantity of informal smuggling continues. The major north-south automobile arteries in North Carolina still have prominent advertisements by price for cigarettes. These ads can only be meant for persons traveling to higher-taxed states.

As can be seen in Table 7.2, federal excise tax receipts fell below state excise receipts in 1970. The federal tax rate had been 8 cents per pack from the 1950s until 1982. While the states had raised the average level of tax from 3 cents per pack in 1954 to 13 cents in 1982, the federal rate had stayed constant. Even though the state tax rose, the combined tax rates did not keep pace with the price level so that the real rate of tax fell from the 1950s to 1980. With the real price of cigarettes falling, consumers would increase the quantity demanded. So, while the government was trying to reduce smoking through the antismoking campaign (that is, shifting the demand curve to the left), it was simultaneously encouraging smoking by pushing consumers down the demand curve.

In 1982, Congress doubled the cigarette tax rate from 8 to 16 cents per pack. The tax was presented as a revenue raising device, although the discouraging effect on smoking was noted. This tax increase was passed while the tobacco industry was going through another upheaval at the farm level. The so called "no net cost tobacco program" was passed by the Congress also. This act changed the nature of the program, so that some of the costs previously borne by government were now to be paid by grower assessments. Also, an equity problem that had arisen between renters and owners of quota production rights had become more intense. The impact on tobacco production of a doubling of the excise tax was therefore of some concern.

A study made by Sumner and Wohlgenant (1982) presents some estimates of this impact. Under very plausible conditions concerning supplies and demands of both products and factors, they concluded that the effect of the larger excise tax on the domestic tobacco price would be quite small—a decline of 3.2 percent at worst. Tobacco itself represents a relatively small fraction of the total cost of cigarettes. The price elasticity of demand for cigarettes is quite small, therefore the quantity of cigarettes demanded will not fall much as a

TABLE 7.5
Effects of the Tobacco Tax Increase

Affected Price or Quantity	Percentage Change
Domestic wholesale price of cigarettes	+18.0
Export wholesale price of cigarettes	−0.3
Domestic quantity of cigarettes	−5.3
Export quantity of cigarettes	+0.9
Import quantity of tobacco	−5.0
Other input quantities	−4.5
Price of U.S. tobacco	−1.5
Domestic use of U.S. tobacco	−4.0
Export quantity of U.S. tobacco	+4.5
Total use of U.S. tobacco	−0.6

Source: Sumner and Wohlgenant 1982.

result of the price increase. Therefore, the impact on tobacco will not be great.

The model that Sumner and Wohlgenant used incorporates the interrelationship among factor demands and supplies, as well as product demand supply. The model does not have to be written out in all its complexity for current purposes. Percentage changes for certain variables are predicted in Table 7.5. These predictions are based on plausible assumptions about certain key parameters. The price decrease for tobacco of 1.5 percent is based on the assumption that the secretary of agriculture will utilize the authority given him to adjust the support price from its formula-dictated level. Examining the model, then, this lower tobacco price should increase exports of U.S. tobacco by 4.5 percent. Thus, even though domestic use of tobacco falls as fewer cigarettes are bought at the 18 percent higher price, the decline is offset by the increased foreign sales.

8

CONCLUDING
REMARKS

The tobacco industry at all levels is the object of governmental intervention, from the elaborate supply control program for the production of burley and flue-cured tobacco to the (usually) large federal and state taxes on tobacco products at the retail level. What this book has attempted to do is to sort out the effects of all these governmental activities on producers of tobacco, manufacturers of products, especially cigarettes, and consumers of those products.

Tobacco has a long history in what is now the United States. It was grown and smoked by the Indians before the English colonies were established. Then the settlers grew it, and it became the main export product of the colonies, the major areas of production being the Maryland and Virginia colonies. Under the colonial system, the grower price of tobacco was no doubt lower than it would have been in a free market system. The gainers in this situation were the crown, through direct taxes, and British merchants, through the exercise of their monopsonistic power.

After independence, tobacco continued to be a major export item for the United States, except for some wartime problems in the first two decades of the nineteenth century. Domestic consumption increased significantly as chewing of tobacco became more socially acceptable in this country. The big change in tobacco use came after the invention and perfection in the 1880s of a cigarette-making machine. Cigarette production and consumption increased rapidly. The Duke family of North Carolina put together a classic interlocking directorate trust. They subsequently changed the trust to a single company in an attempt to avoid the Sherman Anti-Trust Law. They were unsuccessful, however, and the American Tobacco Company was found guilty in 1909 of violating that act. The company was split up into five domestic companies and two foreign subsidiaries.

Each of the five successor companies eventually followed the lead of Reynolds Tobacco Company in promoting a particular brand, leading to fierce competition, through advertising, for market share. Despite this competition, the major tobacco companies were sued once again under the Sherman Act in 1941 for anticompetitive behavior. The companies were charged with colluding to keep up the price of cigarettes and keep down the price of tobacco. Again, the companies were found guilty, and this verdict was upheld by the court. No remedial actions were dictated, and the market structures stayed in place as the cigarette industry entered a new and turbulent era.

In 1933 tobacco was one of the commodities to be included in the original Agricultural Adjustment Act. The supply of tobacco was to be regulated and its price thereby increased. For the next 50 years, with the exception of 1939, there has been a continuous price support program for flue-cured and burley tobacco. In Chapter 3 the various changes in the program over time were chronicled in some detail. Tobacco consumption in the United States peaked in 1953, and per capita consumption of cigarettes peaked in 1963. These dates are interesting since they are obscured by the aggregate data that show cigarette sales rising each and every year. As detailed in Chapter 4, technological change in the production of cigarettes, and later the increased use of filter tips, allowed for more cigarettes to be produced per pound of tobacco. This reduction in the trend demand for tobacco periodically put pressure on the price support–acreage control program. Yields continued to increase, and in some years substantial quantities of tobacco were placed under loan. In 1965 the program was changed to an acreage-poundage program for flue-cured tobacco. For all intents and purposes, the poundage constraint was the operable one. Now quota can be set, and the quantity marketed cannot exceed 10 percent of that quota. This change, which also came about in 1972 for burley, did not alleviate all pressure for the program, but it helped measurably.

Another significant change, especially for flue-cured, was introduced in 1961. This was the within-county lease and transfer program. Previously the only way to acquire allotment was to buy an allotment that went with a given tract of land, or to rent that land and grow tobacco in place. Now quota could be leased and transferred to another site in the same county. In the flue-cured area, this change led to the consolidation of quota into larger operations. Leasing was a necessary step in the mechanization of flue-cured tobacco, a process which is still evolving.

Troubles for the tobacco industry increased greatly in 1964. That was the year of the Surgeon General's Report on Smoking and Health. The report linked cigarette smoking to various serious diseases. As per capita consumption of cigarettes now started declining rather than increasing, added pressure on the supply control program could be predicted.

Another recent activity that has affected the demand of U.S. tobacco is the increase in imported tobacco, both flue-cured and burley. This increase was discussed in Chapter 6. The major cause of the increase seems to be that U.S. leaf with lower stalk position is overpriced. Whatever the reason, the demand curve for domestic leaf has been shifted leftward.

At the time of writing the tobacco industry is in turmoil. Antismoking sentiment, if not increasing, remains high. There is much unrest among the growers, especially in the flue-cured community. The no net cost tobacco program of 1982 is seen as a problem, not a solution. Large amounts of both burley and flue-cured tobacco went into stabilization stocks in 1982. Since allotment holders and growers are responsible now for the financing of the acquisition, processing, and storing of this tobacco, they face much higher assessments for the 1983 crop than they did in the first year of the program. While the burley growers see this as a simple financial burden, the flue-cured community is divided on an equity issue.

As noted above, flue-cured has seen a great deal of consolidation of quota in recent years, as mechanization and bulk curing have become widespread. A grower who wants to expand production can lease quota from a quota holder who does not want to grow tobacco. The lessee can then move the quota to land he owns or rents. The typical lessor might be a widow, a retired farmer, someone with other employment, or previous to the 1982 change, an entity such as a bank or corporation. The typical lessee is a grower with more equipment than he can profitably use on his own quota, and, more importantly, a grower whose skill in tobacco farming leads him to believe that he can generate economic rents to his managerial skills. Since productivity, quality of product, and suitability for machine operations varies among counties, the rent structure for leased and transferred quota is different among counties. In North Carolina, for instance, the eastern section of the state—with preferred soils, flatter terrain, and less nonfarm employment—has higher rents per pound than the piedmont section of the state. The bidding for leased pounds is a market transaction within each county. For several years, growers who were leasing in pounds had bid the price up in certain counties to the point that the expected managerial rents for most growers were bid away. Some growers expressed resentment at this state of affairs. They were probably responsible for the provision in the 1982 legislation requiring nonfarming entities to sell their flue-cured quota. The grower argument that somehow quota should be taken from nongrowers and given to active growers is essentially an attempt to acquire an asset at no cost. The rental price for quota is a market price, and it is the growers themselves who are on the demand side of that market actively bidding up the price.

The no net cost program exacerbated the lessee's feelings. The new rules call for the owner of the quota to pay an assessment in addition to the assessment paid by the grower through a checkoff when he markets the tobacco. Since the increased stabilization receipts called for a reduction in authorized quota, there is less quota available for 1983. As a consequence the rental rate was bid up even higher for the 1983 crop. The growers who believed that they were somehow being treated badly before, now alleged that the owners of quota were including their assessment in their rental offers so that growers would pay both. In a sense this is no doubt true if the growers have bid the rental price up that high. Again, if the rental rate is determined in the market, there is not any equity problem. Both sides of a contract must agree on its provisions. How all this will be resolved is not known, but this internal conflict cannot help the life of the supply control program, which is in trouble from other quarters. We can speculate on two possibilities—the program may be killed by the Congress, and government activity may reduce cigarette consumption further.

The word speculate is used advisedly. Forecasting is a difficult and potentially foolhardy business under the best of conditions. Here we are dealing with political as well as market forces, and traditional microeconomic tools are not sufficient for the task. The problem of curtailing demand was discussed in Chapter 4 and need only be summarized here. The cigarette manufacturers appear to be fully protected against any significant reduction in demand. All of the U.S. firms are now quite diversified, and not so dependent on cigarette sales for revenue. Tobacco farmers would be hurt to the extent that they still had capitalized rents included in their farm values. Their human capital that is specific to growing tobacco would be lost. Many skills and land and certain equipment could be put to other uses. Makers of specialized equipment would be hurt, but total communities are not likely to be irreparably damaged through loss of jobs.

The question of what would happen if the supply control program were eliminated before any drastic change in demand occurred is, perhaps, more interesting. Bills to eliminate the tobacco program have been introduced before, but they appear to be taken more seriously now. The reasoning appears to be that any governmental activity at all that affects production of tobacco is at variance with government policy to discourage smoking. The irony of this position was pointed out earlier. The supply control program restricts production and increases the price of tobacco. Thus consumers use fewer cigarettes than they would if the price were set in a competitive market.

Since the treasury costs for the tobacco program have been quite small compared to other supply control programs, the tobacco program is probably consistent with the anti-smoking campaign. The no net cost program calls for no treasury costs, so that farmers will share with consumers the cost of restricting output, but this still means that cigarette consumption is discouraged at the margin by the program.

If the program were simply abolished, all current holders of quota rights would suffer an immediate capital loss. There is, of course, nothing to prevent Congress from abolishing the program. Some proposed legislation calls for allotment holders to be compensated for their losses. Exactly how this would be accomplished is not clear. Some privately circulated proposals in the flue-cured area call for holders of quota who are not active growers to be required to sell their quota to growers. Since these transactions would be sales, the quota holders would be compensated in such a scheme.

In the burley region there is much less lease and transfer taking place. As explained earlier, burley allotments are typically smaller, and there are not currently any economies of size to exploit. As a consequence, there is not the same equity problem in the burley region as in flue-cured. However, quota holders in burley would face the same wealth loss that flue-cured holders would.

One can speculate about what would happen if the program were ended but tobacco continued to be produced. The location of flue-cured production would no doubt change. Yields and quality are both higher in the sandier areas than they are in the piedmont. Production would move east, and it would probably move south also from Virginia and parts of North Carolina to South Carolina and Georgia. With the passage of time production might even move further, to places like Oklahoma and Texas, or perhaps even California. Burley production might not move, but there certainly would be consolidation of units. Many of the half-acre units would become unprofitable at lower prices.

The prices of both flue-cured and burley would fall. They would fall toward the competitive world market price. United States tobacco would continue to command a quality premium, however, for certain grades. Tobacco prices would become more variable from year to year as the floor price would be removed.

Cigarette manufacturers would see the price of their raw material fall. They might also change their methods of operation. It is likely that some companies might contract directly with growers for tobacco. This would give the buyers more control over quality of leaf. If growers thought that the contracting was one-sided, it is likely that growers of flue-cured, whose number would presumably grow larger, might adopt storage activities of their own. This would even out quantity adjustments even without a stabilization corporation.

None of this may occur at all. The most likely outcome, in the author's judgment, is the following set of actions: Tobacco consumption per capita will continue to fall gradually so that pressure on the program will be less intense. Cigarette manufacturers will sell more beer and other items than cigarettes. This, again, will not be an abrupt move. Congress will continue to juggle the provisions of the supply control program, but will keep it alive. Tobacco in some form will continue to be used. It will not face a sudden death.

BIBLIOGRAPHY

Books

Badger, A.J. 1980. *Prosperity Road.* Chapel Hill: University of North Carolina Press.

Bordeaux, A.F. and Brannon, R.H., eds. 1972. *Social and Economic Issues Confronting the Tobacco Industry in the Seventies.* Lexington, Ky.: College of Agriculture and Center for Development Change.

Buchanan, J., Tollison, R., and Tullock, G., eds. 1980. *Toward a Theory of the Rent Seeking Society.* College Station: Texas A&M University Press.

Finger, W.R., ed. 1981. *The Tobacco Industry in Transition.* Lexington, Ky.: Lexington Books.

Goris, Hendrick. 1954. *Price Determining Factors in American Tobacco Markets.* Amsterdam: North Holland.

Grennes, T., Johnson, P.R., Thursby, M. 1978. *The Economics of World Grain Trade.* New York: Praeger Publishers.

Grubel, H. and Lloyd, P. 1975. *Intra-Industry Trade.* New York: John Wiley and Sons.

Herndon, G.M. 1969. *William Tathan and the Culture of Tobacco.* Coral Gables, Fla.: University of Miami Press.

Jackson, Elmo. 1955. *The Pricing of Cigarette Tobaccos.* Gainesville: The University of Florida Press.

Mann, Charles. 1975. *Tobacco: The Ants and the Elephants.* Salt Lake City, Utah: Olympus Publishing.

Nicholls, William H. 1951. *Price Policies in the Cigarette Industry.* Nashville, Tenn.: Vanderbilt University Press.

Robert, Joseph C. 1967. *The Story of Tobacco in America.* Chapel Hill: University of North Carolina Press.

Rowe, H. 1935. *Tobacco Under the AAA.* Washington, D.C.: The Brookings Institution.

Silberberg, E. 1978. *The Structure of Economics.* New York: McGraw-Hill.

Tennant, Richard. 1950. *The American Cigarette Industry.* New Haven, Conn.: Yale University Press.

Dissertations & Theses

Al-Bandar, T.J. 1966. *The Relationship of Yield Per Acre and Percentage of Tobacco Placed Under Price Support.* M.S. Thesis, North Carolina State University.

Baanante, C.A. 1965. *An Analysis of Certain Aspects of Export Demand for United States Flue-Cured Tobacco.* M.S. Thesis, N.C. State University.

Bordeaux, A.F. 1964. *An Inquiring into the Economic Effects of the Lease and Transfer Program for Flue-Cured Tobacco in North Carolina.* M.S. Thesis, N.C. State University.

Bradford, G.L. 1968. *An Economic Analysis of the Costs of Producing Flue-Cured Tobacco and the Cost Production Variable Relationships.* Ph.D. Diss., N.C. State University.

Brooks, R.C. 1965. *The Potential Demand for United States Flue-Cured Tobacco.* Ph.D. Diss., Duke University.

Capel, R.E. 1966. *An Analysis of the Export Demand for United States Flue-Cured Tobacco.* Ph.D. Diss. N.C. State University.

Cockroft, L.U. 1968. *A Systems Analysis of the Harvesting, Curing, and Marketing States of Flue-Cured Tobacco Production*. Ph.D. Diss., N.C. State University.

Davis, Bob. 1970. *An Economic Analysis of Labor Use for Alternative Flue-Cured Tobacco Harvesting and Curing Systems*. Ph.D. Diss., N.C. State University.

Efstratoglou, S.I. 1968. *The Market for Flue-Cured Tobacco Allotment in North Carolina Under Provisions of the Lease and Transfer Program*. M.S. Thesis, N.C. State University.

————. 1972. *Economic Effects of Inter-County Transfer of Flue-Cured Tobacco Quota*. Ph.D. Diss. N.C. State University.

Evans, D.E. 1981. *An Economic History of the U.S. Flue-Cured Tobacco Program*. M.S. Thesis, N.C. State University.

Harrel, William C. 1975. *An Economic Analysis of Flue-Cured Tobacco Harvesting*. M.S. Thesis, N.C. State University.

Hartman, L.M. 1960. *Influences of Federal Acreage Controls on Costs and Production Practices for Tobacco*. Ph.D. Diss., N.C. State University.

Hendrick, J.L. 1967. *Measurement and Explanation of Factor Returns Under the Flue-Cured Tobacco Program*. Ph.D. Diss., N.C. State University.

Hunt, James B. 1962. *An Economic Analysis of Optimum Flue-Cured Tobacco Production Practices Under Acreage Control and Poundage Control*. M.S. Thesis, N.C. State University.

Lianos, D.P. 1968. *Market Price Variability of Flue-Cured Tobacco by Grades: Seasonal, Geographic and Daily Price Variability*. M.S. Thesis, N.C. State University.

Manning, R.D. 1965. *An Econometric Estimation of the Distributional Impact of the Tobacco Support Program*. Ph.D. Diss., N.C. State University.

May, Robert W. 1970. *An Economic Analysis of Alternative System for Harvesting and Bulk Curing Flue-Cured Tobacco*. M.S. Thesis, N.C. State University.

Moak, S.K. 1966. *Projecting Irrigation of Flue-Cured Tobacco in North Carolina*. Ph.D. Diss., N.C. State University.

Mundy, S.D. 1970. *An Economic Analysis of Five Machine Methods of Transplanting Tobacco*. M.S. Thesis, N.C. State University.

Nicholsen, R.H. 1968. *An Analysis of the Cost of Market Preparation and Market Price Effects of Selling Flue-Cured Tobacco in Tied and Untied Forms at Various Points During the Marketing Season*. M.S. Thesis, N.C. State University.

Norton, Daniel T. 1981. *Institutional Intervention in the Market for an Internationally Traded Commodity: U.S. Flue-Cured Tobacco*. Ph.D. Diss., N.C. State University.

Nuñez, J.F. 1966. *An Analysis of Quantitative Changes in Quality for Flue-Cured Tobacco*. M.S. Thesis, N.C. State University.

Osburn, D.D. 1963. *Factors Influencing the Adoption of Mechanical Harvesting and Curing Techniques by Flue-Cured Tobacco Farmers in Selected Areas of North Carolina*. M.S. Thesis, N.C. State University.

Parker, W.O. 1964. *Efficiency of Farm to Auction Movement of Flue-Cured Tobacco in North Carolina in 1959*. M.S. Thesis, N.C. State University.

Reutlinger, S. 1961. *A Procedure for the Economic Analysis of Irrigation Experiments with an Application to Tobacco and Corn on North Carolina Farms*. M.S. Thesis, N.C. State University.

Stone, Paul S. 1959. *An Economic Analysis of a Two-Row Mechanical Tobacco Harvester*. M.S. Thesis, N.C. State University.

William, Fred. 1980. *Capitalized Allotment Values as Indices of the Uncertainty with which Farmers Perceive Future Tobacco Programs*. Ph.D. Diss., N.C. State University.

Wilson, Ewen, 1973. *An Elasticity Analysis of the Rhodesian Trade Embargo*. Ph.D. Diss., N.C. State University.

Journal Articles

Armington, P.S. 1969a. "A Theory of Demand for Products Distinguished by Place of Production." *IMF Staff Papers* 16 (March): 159–78.

———. 1969b. "The Geographic Pattern of Trade and the Effects of Price Change." *IMF Staff Papers* 16 (July): 179–99.

Harberger, A. 1971. "Three Basic Postulates for Applied Welfare Economics: An Interpretive Essay." *Journal of Economic Literature.* 9(3): 785–97.

Johnson, P.R. 1965. "The Social Cost of the Tobacco Program." *Journal of Farm Economics* 47(21): 242–55.

Johnson, P.R., and Daniel Norton. 1983. "The Social Cost of the Tobacco Program Redux." *Am. Journ. of Agric. Econ.* 65(1): 117–19.

Johnson, P.R., T.J. Grennes, and M. Thursby. 1979. "Trade Models with Differentiated Products." *Am. Journ. of Agric. Econ.* 61(1): 120–27.

Krueger, A.O. 1974. "The Political Economy of the Rent Seeking Society." *Am. Econ. Review* 64(2): 291–303.

Lewit, E.M., D.C. Coate, and M. Grossman. 1981. "The Effects of Government Regulation on Teenage Smoking." *Journal of Law and Economics* 24(3): 545–69.

Lyon, H.L. and J.L. Simon. 1968. "Price Elasticity of Demand for Cigarettes in the United States." *Am. Journ. of Agric. Econ.* 50(4): 888–95.

McKenzie, G.W., and I.F. Pearce. 1982. "Welfare Measurement—A Synthesis." *Am. Econ. Review* 72(4): 669–82.

Mishan, E.J. 1968. "What is Producers Surplus?" *Am. Econ. Rev.* 58(5): 1269–82.

Posner, R.A. 1975. "The Social Costs of Monopoly and Regulation." *Journ. of Political Economy.* 83(3): 807–27.

Reed, Michael. 1980. "An Analysis of Policy Alternatives for the U.S. Burley Tobacco Market." *Southern Journal of Agric. Econ.* 12(2): 71-76.

Schneider, Lynne, B. Klein, and K. Murphy. 1981. "Government Regulation of Cigarette Health Information." *Journal of Law and Economics* 24(3): 575-612.

Seagraves, J.A. 1969. "Capitalized Value of Tobacco Allotments and the Rate of Return to Allotment Owners." *Am. Journ. of Agric. Econ.* 51(2): 320–34.

Sumner, Daniel. 1981. "Measurement of Monopoly Behavior: An Application to the Cigarette Industry." *Journ. of Political Economy* 89(5): 1010–19.

Tullock, G. 1967. "The Welfare Costs of Tariffs, Monopolist, and Theft." *Western Economic Journal* 5(5): 224–32.

Willig, R.D. 1976. "Consumer's Surplus Without Apology." *Am. Econ. Review.* 66(4): 589–97.

Experiment Station Publications

Bordeaux, A.F., D.M. Hoover, and W.D. Toussaint. 1966. "The Lease and Transfer Programs For Flue-Cured Tobacco 1962–1963." Dept. of Econ. N.C. State Univ. AE Information Series no. 129.

Brooks, R.C. 1966. "The Potential Demand for United States Flue-Cured Tobacco." Dept. of Econ. N.C. State Univ. AE Information Series no. 125

Brooks, R.C., and J.C. Williamson. 1958. "Flue-Cured Tobacco Programs 1933–1958." Dept. of Ag. Econ. N.C. State College AE Information Series no. 66.

Bradford, G.L., and W.D. Toussaint. 1962. "Economic Effects of Transferable Tobacco Allotments." Dept. of Ag. Econ. N.C. State College AE Information Report no. 89.

Buccola, S.T., and J.C. Richardson. 1979. "A Quarterly Model of Import Demand for North American Flue-Cured Tobacco." Virginia Polytechnic Institute and State University Research Division Bulletin 147.

Efstratoglou, S., and D.M. Hoover. 1970. "Variability in Rental Rates Paid in the Flue-Cured Tobacco Allotment Rental Markets in Selected North Carolina Counties." Dept. of Econ. N.C. State Univ. ERR 12.

Gibson, W.L., C.J. Arnold, and F.D. Aigner. 1962. "The Marginal Value of Flue-Cured Tobacco Allotments." Agr. Expl. Stat. Va. Polytechnic Institute Technical Bull. 156

Hoover, D.M., and S. Tadalous. 1973. "Economic Effects of Intercounty Transfer of Flue-Cured Tobacco Quota." Dept. of Econ. N.C. State Univ. ERR 23.

Hoover, D.M., and L.B. Perkinson. 1977. "Flue-Cured Tobacco Harvest Labor: Its Characteristic and Vulnerability to Mechanization." Dept. of Econ. and Bus. N.C. State Univ. ERR 38.

Hunt, J.B., W.D. Toussaint, and W.G. Woltz. 1964. "Acreage Controls and Poundage Controls: Their Effects on Most Profitable Production Practices for Flue-Cured Tobacco." N.C. Ag. Exp. Station Tech. Bul. no. 162.

Johnson, Glenn. 1952. "Burley Tobacco Control Programs, Their Overall Effect on Production and Prices 1933–50." Kentucky Agr. Exp. Stat. Bulletin 580.

Johnson, P.R. 1971. "Studies in the Demand for U.S. Exports of Agricultural Commodities." Dept. of Econ. N.C. State Univ. ERR 15.

Johnson, P.R., and R.W. Rudd. 1962. "Effects of the Price Support, Acreage Adjustment and Surplus Removal Program in Dark Tobacco on Kentucky's Agriculture." Kentucky Agr. Exp. Stat. Bulletin 678.

Keller, L., and J. Culver. 1979. "Economic Impacts of Permitting Intercounty Transfer of Burley Tobacco Quotas." Univ. of Tennessee Agric. Exp. Stat. Bull. 589.

Pasour, E.C., W.D. Toussaint, and G.S. Tolley. 1959. "North Carolina Piedmont and Coastal Plain Tobacco Farms: Their Changing Characteristics 1955–1958." Dept. of Ag. Econ. N.C. State College AE Information Report no. 71.

Pierce, W., and M. Williams. 1952. "Cost of Producing Farm Products."
Dept. of Ag. Econ. N.C. State College AE Information Series no. 29.

Pugh, C.R., and R. Collins. 1983. Unpublished farm enterprise budgets.
Dept. of Econ. and Bus. N.C. State Univ.

Pugh, C.R., and D.M. Hoover. 1981. "Lease Rates in North Carolina Counties under the Program for Flue-Cured Tobacco." Unpublished paper,
N.C. State University.

Seagraves, J.A., and R. Manning. 1967. "Flue-Cured Tobacco Allotment
Values and Uncertainty, 1934–1962." Dept. of Econ. N.C. State Univ.
Econ. Res. Rept. no. 2.

Seagraves, J.A., and F.E. Williams. 1981. "Returns to Investors in Flue-
Cured Tobacco Allotments 1975–1980." Dept. of Econ. and Bus. N.C.
State Univ. ERR 42.

U.S. Government

U.S. Dept. of Agriculture. 1950–82. "Annual Report of Tobacco Statistics."
Washington, D.C.: U.S. Government Printing Office.

————. 1960–83. "Tobacco Situation." Washington, D.C.: Economic Research Service.

————. 1982. "Tobacco Market Review, Flue-Cured, 1981 Crop." Agricultural Marketing Service.

U.S. Dept. of Commerce, Bureau of the Census. 1960. *Historical Statistics
of the United States, Colonial Times to 1957.* Washington, D.C.: U.S.
Govt. Printing Office.

U.S. Surgeon General. 1964. "Smoking and Health." Report of the Advi-
sory Committee to the Surgeon General of the Public Health Service,

U.S. Dept. of Health, Education and Welfare. Public Health Service Publication 1103. Washington, D.C.: U.S. Government Printing Office.

Other

Campbell, J. 1981. "American Leaf Exports on Decline: Imperial Tobacco Limited Closes Its Last American Primary Processing Plant." Chapter 13 in Finger, ed.

Hendrick, J.L., G.S. Tolley, and W.B. Back. 1968. "Effect of Flue-Cured Tobacco Programs on Returns to Land and Labor." Econ. Res. Ser., USDA ERS 379

Johnson, P.R. 1972. "The Impact on the Economy of a Decline in Demand for Tobacco." Chapter 13 in Bordeaux and Brannon 1972.

Lemert, B.F. 1939. "The Tobacco Manufacturing Industry in North Carolina." National Youth Administration of North Carolina, Raleigh.

Mann, J. 1974. "Dynamics of the U.S. Tobacco Economy." Econ. Res. Ser. USDA Tech. Bulletin no. 1499.

McElroy, R.C. et. al. 1969. "Potential Mechanization in the Flue-Cured Tobacco Industry with Emphasis on Human Resource Adjustment." Econ. Res. Ser., USDA Agricultural Economic Report no. 169.

Overton, J. 1981. "Diversification and International Expansion: The Future of the American Tobacco Manufacturing Industry with Corporate Profiles of the 'Big Six'." Chapter 15 in Finger, ed.

Pugh, C. 1981. "Landmarks in the Tobacco Programs." Chapter 3 in Finger, ed.

Seagraves, J.A. 1983. "The Life Cycle of the Flue-Cured Tobacco Program." Faculty Working Paper no. 34, N.C. State Univ.

Sumner, D., and M. Wohlgenant. 1982. "Effects of An Increase in the Federal Excise Tax on Cigarettes." Dept. of Econ. and Bus. N.C. State Univ. Faculty Working Paper no. 26.

INDEX

acreage restriction, 33–34, 49
advertising, 22, 61–63, 136
Agricultural Adjustment Act, 26, 31, 33, 55, 136
Agricultural Adjustment Administration, 32
air-cured tobacco, 2, 3
American Tobacco Company, 15, 16, 136
Australia, 110

Belgium, 108
Boeing Aircraft Company, 68–69
Brazil, 110
bright leaf, 7
British American, 15
Brown and Williamson, 15, 20, 21
bulk curing, 84–85
Bull Durham, 8
burley tobacco, 2, 3, 7, 9, 12, 31, 50
Burley Tobacco Growers Association, 35

Camel, 15, 22

Canada, 12, 110, 122
capital, human, 139
cartel, 17, 20, 22
Chesterfields, 15, 22
chewing tobacco, 7, 13, 136
cigar tobacco, 3, 13
cigarettes, and health, 50, 59–61
cigarettes, manufacturing, 13, 14, 136
Civil War, 7
colonial United States, 4–6, 11, 97, 135
Commodity Credit Corporation, 34, 35, 51, 72
Congress, U.S., 33, 139
conscious parallelism, 17
consumer surplus, 26, 28, 56–57
cooperatives, 9, 35, 51
cotton, 8, 67
curing, 84

dark tobacco, 2, 3, 9
differentiated products, 102–3
Duke, 14–15, 136
Dutch auction, 12

elasticities, 24, 114–16, 120–23

153

ABOUT
THE AUTHOR

Paul R. Johnson is Professor of Economics and Business at North Carolina State University, Raleigh, North Carolina. He has previously been associated with the University of Kentucky, the U.S. Department of Agriculture, and the RAND Corporation. He is a co-author of an earlier Praeger Special Studies volume, *The Economics of the World Grain Trade*. He has also published related material in the *American Journal of Agricultural Economics*, the *Economic Record*, the *Southern Economic Journal*, and the *Journal of Econometrics*. Professor Johnson has an A.B. from Oberlin College, an M.S. from North Carolina State University, and a Ph.D. from the University of Chicago.